# PEARL HARBOR

## THE DAY OF INFAMY

# PEARL HARBOR
## THE DAY OF INFAMY

WRITTEN BY
CARL SMITH

COLOR ILLUSTRATIONS BY
ADAM HOOK AND JIM LAURIER

First published in Great Britain in 1999 by Osprey Publishing,
Elms Court, Chapel Way, Botley, Oxford OX2 9LP
Email:info@ospreypublishing.com

Also published as Campaign 62 *Pearl Harbor 1941*

ISBN 1 84176 075 7

Editor: Nikolai Bogdanovic
Design: Black Spot
3D bird's-eye views created by Paul Kime
Maps by Map Studio

Origination by Valhaven Ltd, Isleworth, UK
Printed in China through World Print Ltd.

00  01  02  03  04  10  9  8  7  6  5  4  3  2  1

FOR A CATALOGUE OF ALL BOOKS PUBLISHED BY OSPREY MILITARY,
AUTOMOTIVE AND AVIATION PLEASE WRITE TO:

The Marketing Manager, Osprey Direct USA, PO Box 130,
Sterling Heights, MI 48311-0130, United States of America
Email: info@OspreyDirectUSA.com

The Marketing Manager, Osprey Direct UK, PO Box 140,
Wellingborough, Northants, NN8 4ZA, United Kingdom
Email: info@OspreyDirect.co.uk

Visit Osprey at:
*www.ospreypublishing.com*

## Editor's note

Special thanks go to Ed Chappell of the Pearl Harbor
Survivors' Association; Jim Laurier for his hard work and
intuition; Sid Kennedy, for his expert input on the Kaneohe
attack, and Gordon Jones, another survivor present at the
base on 7 December 1941. Special thanks also to Mr John
Finn, for his patient help in reconstructing the Kaneohe
battlescene. *Aloha* to you all!

## Author's Note

Special thanks are due to the following people: Ray Willis at
RW Books, Manassas, for use of his unpublished photos;
Lou Zocchi, Gamescience, for being a great resource and
for answering those tiring and seemingly endless questions
about research details and aircraft data; Ed Finney and
Jack Green at Naval Historical Photographic Reference
Services for his input on photos and source assistance;
Bob Cresssman at NHCPRS for help on the disposition of
the US Pacific Fleet; Bill Rice for photo reproduction and
enlargement; and Roger Thomas and Bill Gallop for
research assistance. I wish to thank my wife Una for her
patience while I sat cramped with a thousand references
sandbagged around me. This book is dedicated to the men
and women of the nations and forces who were at Pearl
Harbor – may there never be another such war.

## KEY TO MILITARY SYMBOLS

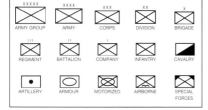

## Key to abbreviations of military ranks

**Adm.** = Admiral
**V.Adm.** = Vice Admiral
**R.Adm.** = Rear Admiral
**Cmdr** = Commander
**Gen.** = General
**Lt.** = Lieutenant
**Cpt.** = Captain

FRONT COVER The battleship *California* took a great deal
of damage from Japanese aircraft. Here she is
photographed from Ford Island as she settles to
the bottom of the harbor.

PAGE 3 **Although most ammunition was kept in the
armory, every barracks bay had centrally located
rifle racks. In theory these racks gave infantrymen
immediate access to their weapons if attacked.**

# CONTENTS

Bored servicemen in Hawaii were always vocal about living conditions or carping about food and barracks life. *A Soldier's Prayer* was circulated at Hawaiian military installations just prior to the attack. After 7 December boredom was forgotten.

LEFT **Pearl was a natural harbor that had been used for over 100 years. An early visitor was the battleship USS *Texas*, shown here with sun awnings in place over the foredeck. In 1940 the Pacific Fleet transferred from California, worrying Japanese military strategists, who saw it as a threat to Japanese security. *Texas* was serving in the Atlantic at the time of the Japanese attack.**

**B**elow, thick fluffy clouds blanketed the blue sky. Shoving the stick forward, Lt. Mitsuo Matazaki dropped his Kate AI-301 beneath them into more blue sky, the horizon broken by the low verdant land mass he was approaching. His observer, Cmdr Mitsuo Fuchida, the mission commander, was watchful. Hawaii looked green and oddly peaceful. He scanned the horizon. It looked too good to be true – other than his fliers, no planes were visible. Fuchida remembered, years later, how peaceful it had appeared.

It was 0730 hrs Hawaii time; the date, 7 December 1941. Fuchida's destination was the home of the US Pacific Fleet – Pearl Harbor. The fleet and three aircraft carriers berthed there were the key targets. A statement notifying the US that war had been declared had been scheduled for delivery to Washington an hour earlier. This air strike would be the first act of war between Imperial Japan and the United States.

All the planning, endless exercises and practice runs would determine the success of this attack. Some military minds thought it would cripple the US fleet; others hoped it might scare the Americans into appeasement; but most felt it would pull Japan into a war with the United States. If war was to be the outcome, some had said, then let it begin here, because Japan's best hope for winning a conflict with the Western giant was to strike first and cripple the US Navy; then Japanese forces could act with a free hand in the following months and further expand their conquests. For Cmdr Fuchida much of this was immaterial, for he was a career officer with a mission: bomb Pearl Harbor.

## POLITICAL BACKGROUND

The Hawaiian Islands lie in the middle of the Pacific, west-south-west of the United States, the first real landfall west of the mainland, positioned at 150°–170° longitude (just east of the International Date Line) and between 18° and 29° north of the Equator. Kauai, Niihau, Oahu, Molokai, Maui, Kahoolawe, Lanai and Hawaii form the major islands in the chain, originally called the Sandwich Islands. The northernmost edge is at roughly the same latitude as Los Angeles, giving the Hawaiian Islands a yearly uniform mild temperature of 75° Fahrenheit and a tropical climate, with cooling ocean breezes, rainforests and dramatic stretches of beach at the foot of majestic mountains and volcanoes. These islands, between Japan and the United States, are a perfect military base, first for naval attack and then for air power.

Hawaii had been discovered by Europeans in the mid-1700s. First ruled by a monarchy, in 1900 it became a US territory, but it was not made a state until 1959. The land is fertile and the beaches, when properly

Despite the war in Europe, in 1941 the US Army was not ready to fight a 'modern' war. Although in 1936-issue field gear, these soldiers on maneuvers would look at home in French trenches a quarter of a century earlier. Note the cloth puttees, campaign hats and gas masks reminiscent of World War I.

BELOW Pearl Harbor was the first stopping point in Pacific Rim waters. Because air power attack was theoretical, Pearl's fortifications relied heavily on coastal guns in heavy positions to defend against naval bombardment.

cultivated, yield immense crops of American, Japanese and international tourists. By the 1930s the population of Hawaii was mostly American and Asian, with its indigenous peoples waning.

Japan took notice of the islands as a potential threat to expansion. Since before the Russo–Japanese War, Japan had been full-steam-ahead modernizing, manufacturing and upgrading its military. With these changes came increased demand for natural resources (steel, oil, gas, raw materials and minerals) and their eyes turned east to China, Indo-China and the islands. Although Russia had traditionally been viewed as the major threat to Japanese expansion and Asian influence, American and European presence in Asia came to the fore.

The Japanese felt European powers were limiting growth of their empire: as Japan expanded, European resistance coalesced which in turn supported Japanese fears of intervention and limitation. Congress placed restrictions on business with Japan and then the majority of the West Coast US fleet made Pearl Harbor its home. Real or imagined, the US fleet posed a threat, and Japan viewed Hawaii with special interest.

The situation worsened as Japan felt strangled and besieged. In Europe when war erupted, and the United States did not intervene as France and Britain became embroiled in conflict with Germany and Italy, Japan noticed. America, it seemed, wanted neutrality: perhaps they would overlook expansions in Asia.

Europeans might have to fight wars on two fronts, but obviously Europe would be their primary theater and the Pacific would occupy a rear seat. The US Pacific Fleet was a deterrent. Japanese and American spheres of influence grew, stretching thinner, threatening to burst. Japan and the United States moved on a collision course: the former needed to grow, the latter wanted to maintain the status quo. Relations worsened, and nationalistic distrust blossomed.

On 7 December 1941 at 0750 hrs the situation exploded. Within hours the United States was no longer neutral.

# OPPOSING COMMANDERS

### Admiral Husband E. Kimmel

Adm. Husband (Hubby) E. Kimmel (1882–1968) was the naval commander at Pearl Harbor in 1941. Born in Henderson, Kentucky, the son of an army major, he graduated from the Naval Academy in 1904. In February 1941 he was promoted over 32 officers to Commander in Chief Pacific (CinCPAC), becoming the navy's senior admiral. Adm. Stark, Chief of Naval Operations (CNO) in Washington, had every confidence in Kimmel's abilities.

As CinCPAC Kimmel moved to Pearl Harbor, home of the Pacific Fleet. Gen. Marshall advised Gen. Short that Kimmel was reasonable and responded well to 'plain speaking'. Kimmel was unhappy with the defense arrangements in Hawaii and at Pearl Harbor. Responsibility for them was split: the army was responsible for land and air defense; the navy for the Navy Yard itself. The navy was responsible for recon-naissance but the army controlled the radar stations and both air and shore defenses in case of invasion. Kimmel let his strong feelings about the tangled web of responsibilities be known.

The US military was understrength and complacent, behind in naval air power and Army Air Corps aircraft, and still thinking of the last war. Weapons, ammunition and manpower were available, but the overriding mentality was that supplies were to be preserved rather than consumed. Kimmel complained to Washington about inequities.

Adm. Kimmel (center) and two members of his staff, his operations officer Cpt. Delaney (left) and his assistant chief of staff Cpt. Smith (right). Although aggressive and vigilant, Kimmel shared responsibility for Pearl Harbor with Gen. Short. Both were surprised by the audacious Japanese thrust at an island almost everyone thought too well defended to be a target.

Without supplies and material, service personnel could not do an adequate job. On top of this, the army and navy competed for allo-cations, and each had its own 'turf' to protect. There was no open rivalry, but clearly the army did not wish to step on the navy's toes and vice-versa, so Kimmel and Short co-operated; but within that inter-service co-operation there was competition and a general lack of sharing any overlapping information. Kimmel was friendly with Short, but each man ran his own show.

Kimmel resented the US policy of building up the Atlantic Fleet at the expense of the Pacific Fleet. The US Navy was a deterrent, but trans-ferring ships and men from the Pacific to the Atlantic affected more than his command – it affected the security of the United States. Still, he was a career officer, and having stated his objections, he followed orders.

Following the events at Pearl Harbor, eight separate investigations of the attack were carried out. The outraged American public reasoned that someone had to be at fault: Kimmel and Short were primarily censured for failure to better co-ordinate and co-operate in the defense of Hawaii. Kimmel retired in March 1942 but went to work as a consultant for a government contractor on secret naval projects.

Blame was fixed on Kimmel and Short: they had been in command when the Japanese struck, and in the minds of many members of the American public, they were responsible. There is a two-year statute of limitations on court martials, and both Kimmel and Short requested one to clear their names, offering to waive the two-year limitation. A court martial before the end of the war was out of the question, partly because of the difficulty of bringing all witnesses together and partly because of the desire to keep secret that the US had broken the MAGIC code.

Kimmel rightly felt he had been made a scapegoat, and in the end the Pearl Harbor investigations revealed that if Kimmel was guilty of anything, it was only of an error of judgment, for which many others, in higher positions, could be similarly censured. However, to many Kimmel was guilty until proven innocent. At first he looked forward to the prospect of a court martial because, he declared, information had been withheld from him which would prove a mitigating circumstance. As time progressed, however, he became bitter and felt betrayed, and when Forrestal finally offered him a court martial in August 1945, he declined, preferring to wait until the Congressional investigation was completed. The final report stated that he was guilty of an error of judgment but not of dereliction of duty. The source of blame was to be found in Washington and Hawaii. Kimmel felt vindicated, but he was unhappy that this had taken several years. He died on 14 May 1968 in Groton, Connecticut.

**American artillery units on Oahu regularly deployed for field maneuvers and war games. Although a strong fortress, many felt the real threat to Oahu was naval bombardment followed by invasion, rather than air attack.**

**Schofield Barracks was the main US Army barracks at Pearl Harbor. Security was not in full force until after the Japanese attack. Note the guardhouses to either side of a swing gate bearing the legend 'Closed'.**

### Major-General Walter C. Short

Maj.Gen. Walter C. Short (1880–1949) was the army commander at Pearl Harbor. Born on 30 March 1880 in Fillmore, Illinois, a doctor's son, he graduated from the University of Illinois and accepted a commission in 1901. A training officer in France in World War One, he later went to Fort Benning as assistant commandant and was promoted to brigadier-general in 1936. He was given command of 1st Infantry Division, and at the outbreak of World War Two, command of 1st Corps. On 8 February 1941 he was promoted to lieutenant-general and given command of the Hawaiian Department.

Short was quiet, dignified and an able organizer. His men were well drilled, but under his command, unit commanders carefully watched the use of expendable ammunition and materiel. Short followed his orders to the letter, but failed to read between the lines. He was surprised when the Japanese attacked Pearl Harbor. Ten days after the attack, he was recalled to Washington and replaced by Gen. Emmons.

The American people were in uproar, and wanted explanations of why the attack had been allowed to happen. Someone had to be at fault; someone had to be responsible. In the rush to judgment and the investigations that followed, Short was considered guilty of failure to co-ordinate the defense of the Hawaiian Islands with Adm. Kimmel. An army investigation found Short derelict in properly directing his staff. The general was quiet, believing that a court martial after hostilities were over and when a full disclosure could be made, would vindicate him.

He reverted to his permanent rank of major-general and retired at the end of February 1942. He accepted the position of traffic manager at the Dallas Ford plant, which made cars and war goods. Although he maintained a low public profile and did not speak with outsiders, he wanted vindication. During the final investigation Short declared that he had not been given adequate warning from Washington and had been suffering from a lack of resources. The investigation revealed that both Washington and Hawaiian commanders had been at fault. Short requested a court martial but never received one. He died on 3 September 1949 in Dallas.

In the 1930s the 'special tractor' light tank was typical of US materiel. It was modeled after the Renault tank and bore too many angled surfaces which would trap shellfire rather than deflecting it. Note the heavy plates instead of treads which were adopted later.

### Admiral Harold R. Stark

Harold (Betty) R. Stark was born on 12 November 1880 in Wilkes-Barre, Pennsylvania, and graduated from Annapolis in 1903. He was befriended by Franklin Delano Roosevelt (FDR) and was awarded the DSM in World War One.

In 1939 Stark became Chief of Naval Operations (CNO) and overcame strong isolationist sentiment to start construction of modern naval vessels and bases. He beefed up the Pacific Fleet at Pearl, and aided by information from the MAGIC code, knew that Japanese–American relations were drastically declining and approaching a state of war. He gave commanders warnings, but because of the belief that Pearl Harbor was too strong, he felt the Japanese would attack elsewhere. When

The unit crest of an artillery unit stationed on Oahu in 1941. Although the motto was 'Take Arms', in general, the army relied upon anti-saboteur and reactive measures more than proactive awareness.

Nomura's message was translated by MAGIC on 7 December 1941, he started to send a message to Pearl Harbor, but Marshall assured him that army communications could get it there just as fast. It arrived after the air raid had begun. Stark was relieved as CNO on 7 March 1942, but Marshall was not removed.

On 1 October 1943 Stark took over command of the 12th Fleet to prepare US Naval Forces for the Normandy invasion; he was liaison with the Admiralty and Churchill. He testified in the Pearl Harbor hearings and retired on 1 April 1946. He died on 20 August 1972 at his home in Washington DC.

### General George C. Marshall

A Kentuckian whose lineage could be traced back to the American Revolution, George C. Marshall was born on 31 December 1880 in Allentown.

Promoted to lieutenant-colonel, he went to France with the AEF, becoming head of operations and training for the 1st Army. He refurbished the army's officer training regiment, implemented Roosevelt's 'CCC' program through the military in the Southern States, and was promoted to chief of war plans and finally deputy to the army's chief of staff.

FDR appointed Marshall chief of staff on 1 September 1939 and gave him his fourth star. Marshall supported the concept of an independent army air corps, and some feel he neglected other branches, building up this new branch at their expense. He was chief of staff when the Japanese attacked Pearl Harbor, but unlike many others, no stigma for the attack was attached to him.

Marshall fully supported the 'defeat Germany first' concept, and many blame the length of the Pacific War upon his cautious approach to planning and implementation of war plans.

After the war he became secretary of state, and he is primarily remembered as the author of the Marshall Plan which reinvigorated Europe. He was awarded the Nobel Peace Prize and died on 16 October 1959.

### Cordell Hull

Lanky and tall, born in a log cabin in Tennessee on 2 October 1871, by his twentieth birthday Cordell Hull had become a circuit judge, through his hard work and diligence.

In 1933 he became secretary of state under FDR. He and Roosevelt became close friends, and although Roosevelt acted as his own secretary of state on most occasions, Hull was a good subordinate and had great influence in matters of foreign policy.

Hull met with Nomura on 7 December 1941: although he probably did believe that the Japanese ambassador had been unaware of the 14-part message until too late, Hull read Nomura the riot act, soundly denouncing the Japanese attack after he had received word of it via chain of command.

Hull tendered his resignation 21 November 1944. He was awarded the Nobel Peace Prize in 1945 and died in 1955.

## President Franklin Delano Roosevelt

Roosevelt, known simply as FDR, is the only American president to have served four consecutive terms, from 1933 until his death in 1945. A distant cousin of Teddy Roosevelt, he graduated from Harvard without distinction. In 1910 he was appointed Secretary of the Navy. In August 1921, while on holiday at Campobello, he was struck with polio, which left him crippled from the waist down, thought he later regained partial use of his legs.

In 1928 Roosevelt was elected governor of New York: four years later he was elected to his first four-year term as president. He established the New Deal conglomerate of economic legislation, designed to help the struggling American economy, and in so doing made himself the champion of the little man.

Although America remained neutral when war broke out in Europe, Roosevelt noted, in a fireside chat on 1 September 1939, that he could not ask all Americans to remain neutral in thought. When Pearl Harbor was bombed, he denounced the action in a speech that decried 7 December as a 'day that will live in infamy'.

He piloted the US through the darkest days of World War Two, but it was too much for him, and he died on 12 April 1945 at Warm Springs, Georgia. His imprint on American political thought remains visible to this day.

## Admiral Isoroku Yamamoto

The seventh son of a schoolteacher, Yamamoto was born 4 April 1884. Isoroku means '56', which was his father's age when he was born. He lived near Nagaoka, entered naval school at 16, and graduated as seventh in his class. He was an ensign on a cruiser in the Battle of Tshushima in the Russo–Japanese War in 1905, when he lost two fingers on his left hand. He was adopted by the Yamamoto family and took their name.

Yamamoto was promoted to commander and transferred to Tokyo naval headquarters, where he married: however, he was sent to Harvard to study economics, and also learned about petroleum. While World War One raged, he discovered the military use of aviation. He was fond of playing go and shogi, and was a guest at many dinner parties, also learning poker and bridge.

In 1923 Cpt. Yamamoto was head of the air training base at Kasumiguara and became naval attaché to Washington. At the London naval conference he convinced all that the 5:5:3 ratio was no longer

President Franklin Delano Roosevelt had already agreed with Britain that the US would abide by a 'defeat Germany first' policy if the US entered the war. The attack on Pearl Harbor would test American resolve.

Fleet Adm. Isoroku Yamamoto was Japan's leading proponent of naval air power and did not wish a prolonged war with the US. He felt Japan could not win, but once Japan entered it, he fought hard for his homeland. Yamamoto was the force behind the Hawaii Operation.

In 1941 artillery units on maneuvers (shown here with unit's terrier mascot) deployed and entrenched using camouflage, in the belief that some day they might have to fight off naval invaders.

acceptable, and it was discarded. He returned to Japan as a diplomatic hero and became Vice-Minister of the Navy.

Yamamoto favored air power, and he relegated the steel navy to a secondary position, opposing the building of the battleships Yamato and Musashi as antiquated technology, saying: 'These … will be as useful … as a samurai sword.' He championed new aircraft carriers, opposed Japan's entry into the Tripartite Pact in 1939, opposed the war hawks, and acknowledged that although he could run wild for six months to a year, after that time he had no confidence whatever in Japan's ability to win a naval war.

In mid-August 1939 he was promoted to full admiral and became commander-in-chief of the Combined Fleet. He became a Rommel-like figure to the men of his command, inspiring them to greater efforts by his confidence, and improved the combat readiness and seaworthiness of the Japanese navy by making them practice in good and bad weather, day and night.

Yamamoto did not wish to go to war with the US, but once the government had decided, he devoted himself to the task of giving Japan the decisive edge. He decided that Pearl Harbor would be won with air power, not battleships. The plan to attack Pearl Harbor was his.

After the success at Pearl Harbor, Yamamoto suffered a defeat at Midway: this has been likened to Lee's early success at Chancellorsville followed by his defeat at Gettysburg. Some have speculated that he was overconfident. During the battle for Guadalcanal, he decided to visit his men to inspire confidence and improve morale. His plane was shot down on 18 April 1943 by American fighters.

His death deprived the Japanese military not only of a courageous and insightful leader, but of a man who was a true military professional, a man who fought but wanted peace. Had he lived, the outcome of the war would probably not have changed: however, his stature and efforts might have shortened the struggle.

In early 1941 army issue equipment was far behind where it would be a scant five years later. Bolt action Springfields, old gas masks, and 'dishpan' helmets would shortly be replaced when war production went into high gear.

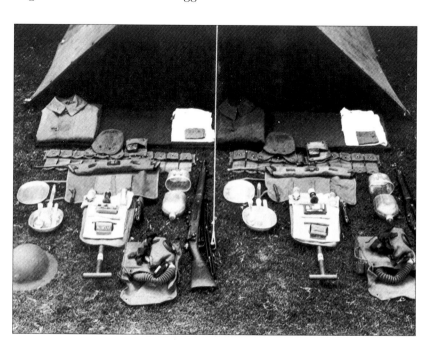

## Commander Mitsuo Fuchida

Born in Nara Prefecture on 2 December 1902, in the Year of the Tiger, Mitsuo Fuchida was clever, outspoken and personally fearless. In 1921 he entered the Naval Academy and shortly thereafter befriended Minoru Genda when they discovered a shared love for flying. Their friendship and mutual respect was to last for years, and in many ways it helped shape the concept of air war and the attack on Pearl Harbor. Somewhat ironically, he once characterized his friend Genda as 'reckless'.

First specializing in horizontal bombing, Fuchida gained such prowess that he was made an instructor. Shortly thereafter he was promoted to lieutenant-commander and was accepted into the Naval Staff College. It was there that he espoused naval air power.

In 1939 he joined the *Akagi* as flight commander. On sea exercises he met Adm. Yamamoto, who expressed his real interest in naval aviation. Fuchida came to respect Yamamoto and became a devoted supporter of the admiral. After a short stint on *Ryuho*, he returned to *Akagi* with more than 3,000 hours of flight time under his wings. While in China, he learned the art of torpedo bombing, and when he returned to *Akagi*, he was recognized throughout the IJN as a torpedo ace.

Fuchida was a hard-headed officer who tenaciously defended an idea until it was proven untenable; then he compromised. He had a sly sense of humor, defended the underdog, and was a kind, gentle man in private life, but he had the spirit of a warrior. Nicknamed 'Buddha' by his friends for his good humor, he was an officer who planned things down to the last detail, had insight into tactical and strategic situations, and was personally brave and respected by his men. Genda once said of him:

**Sunday morning on 7 December 1941 at Ford Island would have looked as peaceful as this shot, taken barely four weeks earlier. Note *Lexington* (CV2) on the west side of the island (top of picture) and Battleship Row on the east side (bottom of picture). Japanese intelligence regularly scoured newspapers for word of naval comings and goings.**

'He was … our best flight leader … with a clear head. The success of the Pearl Harbor attack depended upon the character and ability of its flight leader, and that is why Fuchida was selected for the job.'

He co-ordinated all preparations for the attack on Pearl Harbor and personally led the first wave, flying as an observer with Lt. Mitsuo Matazaki. He wanted to conduct a second attack against Pearl Harbor, but Nagano decided they had done well enough and turned the task force home.

Fuchida met the Emperor face to face and provided details of the assault on Pearl Harbor: later he said it was easier to go into combat than to face him then. Sidelined at Midway by appendicitis, Fuchida was soon back to duty and was active throughout the remainder of the war. Afterwards he converted to Christianity, became a minister, and wrote about the Pearl Harbor attack. He died in 1976.

### Commander Minoru Genda

Born in 1904, Genda attended the naval training school and shortly afterwards met Mitsuo Fuchida. Genda served in the oldest Japanese fighter squadron, the Yokosuka Air Group, under Lt. Kobayashi. Their aerial acrobatics quickly gained the group the sobriquet 'Genda's Circus'. He was recognized as a superior fighter pilot and air operations officer.

R.Adm. Onishi had Genda write a feasibility study for a proposed Japanese attack on Pearl Harbor. Cmdr Genda wrote the study and with Cmdr Mitsuo Fuchida constructed a strategy with ten main points, most of which were incorporated into the final plan. He developed the First Air Group's torpedo program, and proposed a second attack on Pearl Harbor several days after the first, wanting to annihilate the US Fleet. He remained aboard (*Akagi*) as Nagumo's air advisor, and was on deck to welcome Fuchida's flight back.

Genda was important in the Midway attacks, taking Fuchida's place in the squadron since the latter was recuperating following his operation. Later he was promoted to captain and posted as senior officer in charge of naval aviation on the general staff. When Air Group 343 formed in December 1944, Genda transferred from general staff to become its commander. He stressed formation combat, improved air-to-air communications, and advance intelligence of enemy air formations. He led the group in the Battle of Okinawa, and commanded Air Group 353 until the end of the war.

### Vice-Admiral Chuichi Nagumo

Chuichi Nagumo was born in 1887. Of fiery temperament, this career naval officer was an expert in torpedo warfare. His military stratagems were often aggressive but uninspired and sometimes ill-advised. V.Adm. Nagumo was appointed commander of Kido Butai, the 1st Air Fleet, despite his lack of familiarity and experience in naval aviation.

He commanded the 1st Air Fleet at Pearl Harbor from the deck of his flagship, *Akagi*. Three attack waves were planned, but after the first two, he called off the third, deciding that it would not yield any further results and that the Americans were now somewhat prepared and would probably inflict disproportionate casualties on the attack force.

Subsequent events have shown that it probably would have further crippled US ability to strike back.

Afterwards he led the 1st Air Fleet in the Dutch East Indies, the Indian Ocean and at Midway, where he lost *Akagi*, *Kaga*, *Hiryu* and *Soryu*, four of Japan's finest carriers, because of poor tactical ability and bad luck. The magnitude of this loss disconcerted him. Afterwards he lost his drive and any effectiveness he possessed as a commander. As a subordinate of Adm. Kondo he helped achieve the Japanese tactical victory (but strategic defeat) at Santa Cruz.

At Saigon in 1944 he commanded a backwater fleet of barges, patrol boats and infantry. When the inevitable result of the war became clear, he committed suicide, on 6 July 1944.

### Ambassador Kichisaburo Nomura

Adm. Kichisaburo Nomura was the Japanese ambassador to Washington during Pearl Harbor, and was cast unwittingly in the role of villain.

Born in 1877, he was orphaned, and later adopted by Masatane Nomura, taking his name. In 1898 he graduated from the Naval Academy with imperial honors for scholarship. He commanded the 3rd Fleet during the 1932 Shanghai Incident, coming through the conflict unscathed only to lose his left eye to a terrorist bomb just weeks afterwards.

Nomura retired from active duty but served as foreign minister in the government from 23 September 1939 to 14 January 1940. His was a voice of constraint and caution, encouraging diplomatic solutions.

In February 1941 Nomura was sent to the United States as ambassador to Washington. As he opposed Japanese militarists, he was welcomed and trusted when he tried to reconcile US–Japanese differences with Cordell Hull.

Both Hirohito and Yamamoto insisted that at least 30 minutes notice be given the US prior to the outbreak of hostilities at Pearl Harbor. A message was sent to Nomura: he was to give it to Hull at one o'clock Washington time. The message was sent in 14 parts and decoded as it arrived. Because of difficulties sending it, Nomura did not have the entire message, and postponed his appointment until 1400 hrs. However, the US had broken the code and was confused about the intent of the message because it neither declared war nor offered hope of peace through further negotiations.

Nomura saw Hull at 1420 and delivered the incomplete message. Hull was infuriated and terse during the meeting. Nomura soon found the reason for Hull's reception: Pearl Harbor had been attacked by Japan. Hull declared to the press immediately afterwards that he had never seen a message so full of 'falsehoods and distortions … on a scale so huge that I never imagined … any government … was capable of uttering them'. Nomura was shaken by the revelation that Japan had attacked the US, and shoulders sagging he left Hull's office.

Nomura and his staff were interned, and remained so until 1942, when he was repatriated. After the war he became president of the Japan Victor Company and was a member of the House of Councilors. He died in 1964.

# CHRONOLOGY

## 1936

**2 December** Yamamoto begins forging the naval air arm into a modern weapon.

## 1939

**10 February** Japan occupies the Chinese island of Hainan.
**August** Adm. Isoroku Yamamoto appointed commander-in-chief of the Japanese Imperial Navy.
**4 September** Yamamoto writes to V.Adm. Shimata to say that he is uneasy about 'Japan's relations with Germany and Italy in the face of changes now taking place in Europe'.

## 1940

**Spring** The US fleet transfers to Pearl Harbor as its permanent home base: to the Japanese, this is a thinly veiled threat. Yamamoto uses this to urge expansion of naval air power. Yamamoto begins thinking that it would be better to carry war to the US Navy rather than wait for them to choose the time and place for battle.
**July** Roosevelt has an embargo placed on all aviation fuel, steel and scrap iron to Japan.
**August** Lt.Col. Friedman, a cryptographer, breaks the Japanese Code Purple (MAGIC) code.

**View of South-East Loch, looking north from the Hickam Field side, where sub pens and PT berths were located (to right). Battleship Row is out of sight to the left. Mountains, destroyer berths and Pearl City are faintly visible in the background.**

**3 September** Roosevelt gives Britain 50 old destroyers for the rights to establish US naval bases in British territories.

**4 September** The US warns Japan not to attack French Indochina.

**11 September** Ojiro Okuda is appointed acting consul general to Hawaii. He is in charge of reporting on movements of US ships in the harbor, much of which appears in American newspapers. Kohichi Seki studies *Jane's Fighting Ships* and travels around the island studying the base and airfields, without trespassing on US government property though.

**27 September** Japan joins the Tripartite Pact. Yamamoto tells Konoye: 'I hope you will … avoid a Japanese–American war'.

**12 November** British torpedo bombers attack the Italian fleet at Taranto, disabling half of Italy's Mediterranean fleet.

**10 December** Yamamoto writes to Shimada: 'The probability is great … our operations against the Netherlands' Indies are almost certain to develop into a war with America, Britain and Holland before those operations are half-over. Consequently we should not launch … the southern operation unless we are prepared … and adequately equipped.'

**30 December** R.Adm. Block sends a memo: 'Any aircraft attacking Pearl Harbor will … be brought by carriers.'

# 1941

**1 January** In Japan, American ambassador Grew writes in his diary: 'Japan … is on the warpath … If … Americans … could read … articles by leading Japanese … they … would realize the utter hopelessness of a policy of appeasement.'

**6 January** President Roosevelt declares the United States the 'arsenal of democracy'.

**7 January** Yamamoto writes a letter to R.Adm. Takijiru Oikawa, saying: 'A conflict with the United States … is inevitable.' The Japanese navy should 'destroy the US main fleet at the outset of the war'. He continues that the Japanese Navy should strike so as to 'decide the fate of the war on the very first day'. His plan is to find the US Navy 'at Pearl Harbor [and] attack it vigorously with our air force'. He concludes that if the US Navy is not at Pearl Harbor, they should find them regardless of where they are. The Japanese First and Second Carrier Divisions should mount a 'surprise attack with all their air strength, risking themselves on a moonlight night or at dawn'. Oilers were needed for at-sea refueling, destroyers would pick up survivors whose aircraft or ships went down, and submarines would attack vessels fleeing Pearl Harbor and attempt to sink allied vessels at the entrance and block it. An attack on 'the Philippines and Singapore should be made at almost the same time as … against Hawaii'. At the end of the letter, Yamamoto requests: 'I sincerely desire to … personally command that attack force.'

**24 January** Prince Fumimaro Konoye, the Japanese prime minister, asserts that 'firm establishment of a Mutual Prosperity Sphere in Greater East Asia is … necessary to the continued existence of this country'. Yamamoto hypothesizes that should war break out 'between Japan and the United States, it would not be enough that we take

**In late October Ford Island (center), the tank farm on the South-East loch (center left, opposite Ford Island) and Hickam Field (top left) were business-as-usual bases. War was in Europe or China.**

Guam and the Philippines, nor even Hawaii and San Francisco. We would have to … dictate the terms of peace in the White House. I wonder if our politicians … are prepared to make the necessary sacrifices'.

**27 January** In secret talks with Britain the US decides that if Japan enters the war on the German side, and if the US enters the war, Germany is to be defeated first, then Japan. Ambassador Grew in Japan is warned by his Peruvian counterpart that he has heard a Japanese worker in his embassy say that if war occurs the 'Japanese military … [will] attempt a surprise mass attack on Pearl Harbor using all their military facilities'. In Washington military intelligence is surprised only that Grew puts credence in the source of the report and not in the supposition of the report. In Japan, Foreign Minister Yosuke Matsuoka says 'We must control the Western Pacific' and that the US should reconsider their prior actions: if the US does not, there is 'no hope for Japanese–American relations'. Aboard *Nagato*, Yamamoto discusses the logical and technical feasibility of an attack on Pearl Harbor. After this meeting Onishi asks Maeda (his senior staff officer) the following question: if US capital ships were 'moored around Ford Island, could a successful torpedo attack be launched against them?' Maeda says no, the water is too shallow for torpedoes to be effective. However, if the torpedoes were modified…

**1 February** Kimmel replaces Richardson as CinCPAC; Short is promoted to commander of the Hawaiian Department.

**5 February** Kimmel receives a letter from Secretary Knox stating: 'If war eventuates with Japan … hostilities … would start … with a surprise attack on Pearl Harbor.' The letter tells Kimmel to 'increase the joint readiness of the army and navy to withstand a raid'. He says that probable forms of attack are bombing, torpedo attacks, or both. Congressman Faddis of Pennsylvania states: 'The Japanese are not going to risk a fight … where they must face the American Navy in open battle. Their navy is not strong enough.'

**12 February** Nomura presents his credentials to Cordell Hull, which appoint him Ambassador to Washington.

**15 February** Kimmel issues a Pacific Fleet Conference letter saying they are faced with a possible surprise attack on ships in Pearl Harbor.

**Mid-February** Onishi sends for Cmdr Minoru Genda and presents Yamamoto's plan, mentioning that Yamamoto has given some thought to making it a one-way mission (*katamechi kogami*) to increase the striking distance to over 500 miles. Genda opposes treating aircraft as disposable: 'Ditching … would be a waste of men and planes.' He thinks Yamamoto should include dive-bombers and high altitude bombers as well as torpedo planes in the attack. 'To obtain the best results, all carriers should approach as close to Pearl Harbor as possible.' His last point is: 'Our prime target should be US carriers.' Onishi asks Genda to prepare a report about feasibility, component forces and manner of execution, and then report back in ten days.

**Late February** Genda gives Onishi a report containing ten main proposals. It must be a surprise attack; US carriers are its main objective; US aircraft on Oahu are an objective; and every available Japanese carrier should take part in the operation. Furthermore, all kinds of attack aircraft should be used, and Japanese fighters should play an active role in the attack; the attack should be in early morning; refueling vessels at sea is necessary for success; and all planning must be ultra-secret. The tenth proposal is for a full-scale invasion, which Onishi disagrees with because they could not maintain supply so far from their present bases. Yamamoto wants to cripple the US Navy whereas Genda feels they should annihilate it.

At the time of the attack on Pearl Harbor, the Army Air Force still had some old and obsolete aircraft such as this twin-engine Dolphin amphibian.

**27 February** Okida reports: 'The fleet goes to sea for a week and stays in Pearl Harbor for one week. Every Wednesday those at sea and those in the harbor change places.'

**5 March** The Japanese foreign ministry wires Nomura to say that they feel fairly certain that the US 'is reading your code messages'.

**10 March** Onishi gives Yamamoto a draft of his plan for attack, based on Genda's plan but with some modifications.

**11–12 March** Congress passes the Lend Lease Act, which supplies materiel to governments fighting the Axis.

**14 March** Kita is appointed consul general to Hawaii.

**20 March** Nomura responds to the foreign ministry: 'Though I do not know which ones, I have discovered that the United States is reading

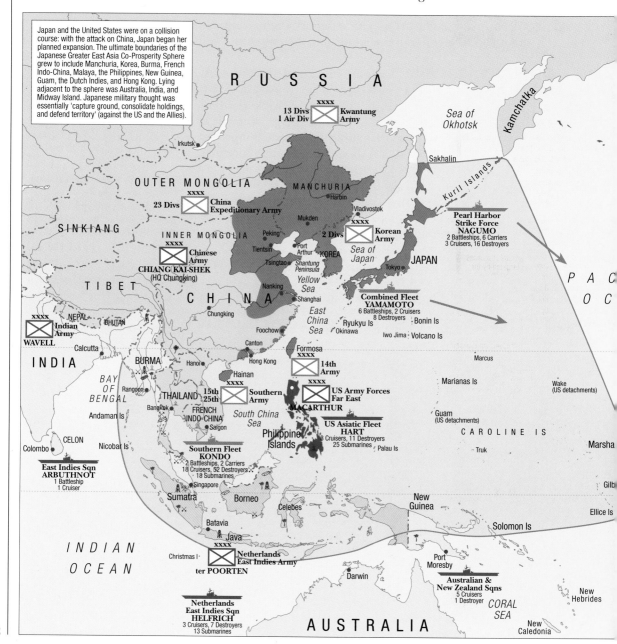

Japan and the United States were on a collision course: with the attack on China, Japan began her planned expansion. The ultimate boundaries of the Japanese Greater East Asia Co-Prosperity Sphere grew to include Manchuria, Korea, Burma, French Indo-China, Malaya, the Philippines, New Guinea, Guam, the Dutch Indies, and Hong Kong. Lying adjacent to the sphere was Australia, India, and Midway Island. Japanese military thought was essentially 'capture ground, consolidate holdings, and defend territory' (against the US and the Allies).

some of our codes.' Nomura informs them he will tell them details in a 'safe' way. Still they did not change the Purple Code. Matsuoka may have been suspicious of Nomura's warning, feeling it sprang from insecurity.

**27 March** Takeo Yoshikawa, an intelligence officer, arrives in Pearl Harbor and realizes that battleships are berthed in pairs and that the in-shore ship is protected from torpedo attacks by the outboard one.

**30 March** Roosevelt orders the Coast Guard to seize two German, 28 Italian and 35 Danish ships in US ports.

**1 April** Naval Intelligence in Washington alerts district commanders to the fact that 'the Axis Powers often … [attack on] Saturday and Sunday or on national holidays' and that commanders should put 'proper watches and precautions … in effect'.

**10 April** The IJN reorganizes into the 1st Air Fleet, with the First Carrier Division (*Kaga* and *Akagi* and four destroyers), the Second Carrier Division (*Hiryu* and *Soryu* and four destroyers) and the Fourth Carrier Division (*Ryuho* and two destroyers).

**13 April** Japan and Russia sign a neutrality pact giving Japan the green light for southward expansion.

**15 April** The US begins shipping lend-lease goods to China.

**21 April** US, English and Dutch officers co-ordinate the proposed roles of each in the military defense against Japan in case of a Japanese attack on Singapore.

**23 April** Marshall disagrees with Roosevelt's decision to keep the US fleet in Hawaii because 'our heavy bombers and … pursuit planes … could put up such a defense that the Japs wouldn't dare attack Hawaii'.

**28 April** When queried about the US choice to strengthen the Atlantic Fleet by removing vessels from the Pacific, the British reply that the 'reduction … would not unduly encourage Japan'. *New Mexico, Mississippi, Idaho, Yorktown,* four light cruisers, 17 destroyers, three oilers, three transports and ten auxiliaries are transferred by the end of summer.

**20 May** Nomura confirms to Tokyo: 'the US is reading some of our codes'.

**26 May** Yoshikawa reports that three battleships and three light cruisers have disappeared from Pearl Harbor. Kimmel fires off an 11-page memo noting that 72 per cent of the new officers for the Atlantic came from the Pacific Fleet and that the Pacific Fleet's needs are sub-ordinated to those of Britain and the Atlantic Fleet.

**27 May** Roosevelt declares the US to be in an unlimited state of national emergency.

**14 June** The US freezes German and Italian assets.

**16 June** German consulates in the US are shut down.

**17 June** Germany moves against US property in Germany.

**20 June** The US stops oil shipments from Gulf and East Coast ports to all destinations except Latin America and Britain.

**22 June** Italian consulates in the US are closed.

**26 June** Vichy France permits Japan to occupy French Indochina. The US impounds Japanese credits in the US. Roosevelt nationalizes the Philippine Army.

**17 July** A new Japanese government is formed.

**28 July** The US puts an embargo on oil sales, freezes assets and closes ports to Japanese vessels.

BELOW **Planned boundaries of the Japanese Greater East Asia Co-Prosperity Sphere.**

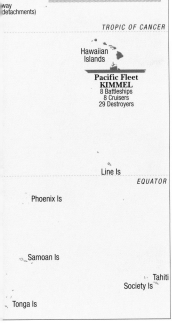

British Possessions
United States
Dutch
Japanese Empire 7 Dec. 1941
Greater East Asia Co-Prosperity Sphere

Rubber
Oil
Coal
Gold
Lead
Tin
Rice
Hemp
Opium
Natural resources targeted by the Japanese

*TROPIC OF CANCER*

Hawaiian Islands

**Pacific Fleet**
**KIMMEL**
8 Battleships
8 Cruisers
29 Destroyers

Line Is

*EQUATOR*

Phoenix Is

Samoan Is

Tahiti
Society Is

Tonga Is

**18 August** An amendment to the 1940 Selective Service Law extends the length of service for US inductees from one year to two-and-a-half years.

**24 September** A message from Tokyo to the Consulate General instructs spies to report on US vessels in Pearl Harbor.

**16 October** Konoye resigns and Gen. Tojo sets up a new government with himself as prime minister. Stark warns Kimmel of the possibility of Japanese activities.

**5 November** Yamamoto issues Top Secret Order No.1 to the Combined Fleet, detailing the plan for the attack on Pearl Harbor.

**7 November** Congress repeals sections of the Neutrality Act concerning arming US cargo ships and transporting war goods to warring nations.

**10 November** Britain states that should Japan go to war with the US, they will declare war on Japan 'within the hour'.

**22 November** The US intercepts a message telling Nomura that the deadline of 22 November has been extended to 25 November 1941.

**25 November** No US–Japanese agreement is reached: consequently, Nagumo's task force sails from the Kuriles.

**27 November** Argentina decides not to sell tungsten to Japan. Kimmel and Short are advised that US–Japanese negotiations have failed and that they should be prepared for any eventuality. Kimmel is ordered to deliver 25 aircraft to Wake and Midway.

**2 December** Nagumo gets the go-ahead. The US intercepts a message to the Japanese Embassy to destroy all codes.

**6 December** Roosevelt is given the partly deciphered 14-part message. Instructions state it is not to be given to Hull until 1300 hrs Washington time on 7 December.

**7 December** The Japanese Navy attacks Pearl Harbor.

**8 December** Roosevelt calls the attack on Pearl Harbor a day that will 'live in infamy', and Congress declares war on Japan. Gen. Yamashita's 25th Army lands near the borders of Thailand and Malaya and begins the battle for Singapore.

**11 December** Italy and Germany declare war on the US.

**12 December** Japanese forces occupy Guam.

**23 December** Japanese forces capture Wake Island.

**25 December** Hong Kong falls to the Japanese.

# 1942

**15 February** Singapore surrenders.

# THE JAPANESE PLAN

J apan expanded into Asia. US–Japanese relations declined and an embargo on Japanese products sent diplomatic efforts spiraling downward. Ambassador Nomura was appointed and officials hoped he could mend a brittle friendship.

The Japanese government favored controlling Asia's natural resources in what was known as the Southern Resource Area. Japan's treaty with Russia protected her from advances on that front: she already controlled Manchuria, Korea, the eastern third of Mongolia, Shanghai, Formosa and French Indo-China by mid-1941; and now Europe was unable to interfere effectively. The area under Japanese control was called the Greater East Asia Co-Prosperity Sphere. Gen. Hideki Tojo formed a new government, with himself as prime minister and the military (primarily the army) in control.

Ambassador Nomura met repeatedly with Cordell Hull in attempts to reach a solution. Japan would settle for nothing less than the Co-Prosperity Sphere, and negotiations slowed to a standstill. Although neutral, the US thwarted every Japanese attempt to extend Asian influence. With hawks controlling the Japanese government, perhaps Japan could negotiate with the US, but if not, then they would start a *blitzkrieg*, and when things settled down, they would control the territories they wanted. With European powers occupied, war in Asia would be an unwelcome second front. Nomura had a deadline for diplomatic success which was also the deadline for commencement of a Pacific offensive. Japanese contingency plans would kick in if negotiations with the United States collapsed. The Japanese watched the expansion of Pearl Harbor with considerable interest and concern.

**The Japanese hoped to catch the US carriers *Lexington*, *Saratoga* and *Enterprise* at Pearl Harbor. *Saratoga* was at San Diego and *Enterprise* was delivering planes to Wake and *Lexington* to Midway when the Japanese struck.**

The Japanese held a theory of the 'Great All-Out War' with the US Navy. The roots of this near mythical theory lay in their great victories of Port Arthur and Tsushima, where the Japanese Navy had defeated the Russian fleet. According to the theory, warships led by battleships would steam towards one another in a sea battle the like of which had not been seen since Trafalgar. Japanese warships had been thoughtfully designed to better their American counterparts either with an extra gun, extra speed, more torpedo tubes or anything else which gave each vessel an edge on its opposing number. The Japanese Navy trained under the notion that America was the biggest threat they faced, and that when the smoke of battle drifted away, the Rising Sun would be victorious.

1. 07 December 1941: The US Pacific Fleet is attacked in Pearl Harbor.
2. 07 December 1941: Midway Island is shelled by destroyers *Ushio* and *Sazanami*.
3. 08 December 1941: Gen. Yamashita's 25th Army invades Malaya.
4. 08 December 1941: US garrison in Shanghai is overrun by Japanese troops.
5. 08 December 1941: Singapore is bombed in the early hours.
6. 09 December 1941: Japanese troops occupy Taraw and Makin on the Gilbert Islands.
7. 09 December 1941: Bangkok falls to the Japanese.
8. 10 December 1941: The British ships *Repulse* and *Prince of Wales*, part of Strike Force Z, are sunk off Malaya by Japanese aircraft.
9. 11 December 1941: The small US garrison in Peking is overrun by the Japanese. The troops there are taken prisoner.
10. 13 December 1941: Gen. Homma's 14th Army (43,000 troops) invades the Philippines.
11. 16 December 1941: Japanese forces begin the invasion of Borneo, landing in Sarawak and Brunei.
12. 23 December 1941: The Japanese capture Wake Island.
13. 24 December 1941: Further Japanese landings take place south of Manila, from the Palau Islands.
14. 25 December 1941: Hong Kong falls. Three Japanese divisions take the city, inflicting numerous casualties.
15. 11 January 1942: Japanese troops land on Celebes Island: war on the Dutch East Indies is formally declared the following day.
16. 15 January 1942: Gen. Iida's 15th Army begins the invasion of Burma.
17. 23 January 1942: Japanese invasion of New Guineau begins. Vice-Adm. Nagumo's 1st Air Fleet and Adm. Inouye's 4th Fleet spearhead the attack.
18. 24 January 1941: Four US destroyers attack a Japanese convoy in the Makassar Strait, inflicting considerable damage.

The Japanese attack was well planned and the targets plotted. This contemporary map was captured from a Japanese two-man sub. Note the chart is in English, the notations Japanese.

BELOW **The Japanese tidal wave, 7 December 1941 to 31 January 1942.**

The Japanese task force and submarine forces that attacked Pearl Harbor on 07 December 1941 approached using different routes, before co-ordinating the final attack off the Hawaiian Islands. However, this action was only part of the larger pan-Pacific activity that sought to settle the boundaries of the Greater East Asia Co-Prosperity Sphere. The months following 07 December 1941 were to witness a sequence of movements intended to significantly shift the power balance in the Pacific, and increase Japan's imperial dominion.

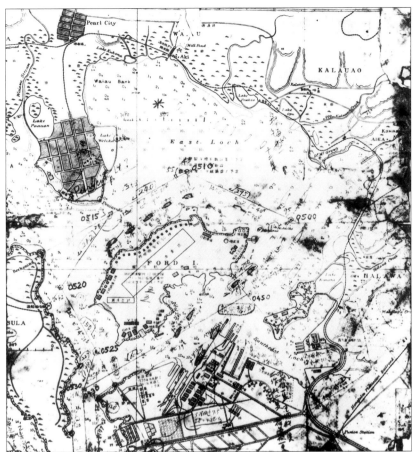

Within the Japanese Navy there was a rift between the battleship admirals and the younger air power admirals: the former held true to the Great All-Out War theory, while the latter realized that British success at Taranto presaged the future of naval warfare. Yamamoto trained young officers of the Japanese Navy for air war.

In early 1941 Yamamoto began preparation for the Southern Operation, the Japanese plan to conquer the resource-rich areas of Asia. One of the operation's components, the Hawaii Operation, comprised the thrust on Pearl Harbor. Plans were clear: if negotiations had not succeeded by 23 November 1941, a military solution would commence. A code tied to weather forecasts was devised and legations were notified. If the weather report called for 'east wind, rain', it meant US–Japanese negotiations had broken down and code machines in the United States were to be destroyed in preparation for war. That message also gave the Hawaii Operation task force a green light to attack.

The Japanese Navy had details on Pearl Harbor. As the harbor was in plain view of the city, and visitors could take aerial sight-seeing trips over the naval basin and near most military posts, espionage was a matter of looking, recording and keeping track of naval traffic, as opposed to sneaking onto military reservations. Within a few months a spy at the Japanese embassy had a complete record of all vessels stationed at Pearl, their schedules, which ships were under repair, which had left for sea duty and the disposition of aircraft. The spy passed Tokyo this information.

Some destroyers and smaller vessels at Pearl could berth dockside. When doing so, they ran power lines to shore and often shut down their boilers so only minimal power was available: this delayed them from getting underway when attacked.

Alerted by Washington, Kimmel and Short passed the order for extra vigilance on 27 November. Hawaii was easy duty and, if the truth were known, somewhat dull, as are most routine peacetime military stations. Men complained about the food, the weather, pay-day, duty rosters and so on. War seemed distant from Hawaii.

Still, Gen. Short was concerned about sabotage, and he ordered all army aircraft to be bunched together so they could better be guarded: however this also made them sitting ducks for an air assault. He ordered munitions secured, coastal artillery put on alert and radar stations shut down at 0700 hrs. Adm. Kimmel started rotating carriers in and out of the harbor and set up ship and naval aircraft patrols. Vessels were alert for submarine threats to shipping. The aircraft carrier *Lexington* was ordered to take aircraft which Kimmel felt were sorely needed at Pearl to Midway. Despite precautions, no one really dreamed of an air attack. Warships, yes; sabotage and possibly an invasion force, yes; but air attack? No one gave it much credence.

US government cryptographers monitored Japanese transmissions. Washington, while still neutral, agreed with London that the Allies would concentrate on defeating Germany first. London was given three of the ultra-secret MAGIC decoders, but Pearl Harbor did not receive any. Moreover, because of the 'defeat Germany first' mentality, men and materiel which could have bolstered the Pacific were diverted to the Atlantic. 50 lend-lease destroyers which the US Navy could have readily used were sent abroad.

Despite the shadow of war, life went on as usual in Pearl Harbor. Generally speaking, ships on maneuvers returned in time to spend the weekend at their berths in the harbor. Although supposedly a third of the fleet was out at any one time, sometimes comings and goings over-

Oahu was the first leg of the journey for the China Clipper. Like many of the military amphibians or seaplanes, the Clipper was moored in shallow waters adjacent to shore. Japanese intelligence was so good that the Clipper was not attacked during the air assault.

lapped. Pearl Harbor was the strongest base in the Pacific, and the first way-station from the mainland to the Orient. Artillery protected the coastline, and although some older aircraft were there, newer B-17s flew in regularly from the US. Japan viewed Pearl Harbor as the number one threat to security.

### Opening moves

Although he did not know the significance of the date, Nomura was told to complete negotiations by 22 November. He requested an extension from Tojo and was told: 'There are reasons beyond your ability to guess why we want to settle Japanese–American relations by the 25th.' The message granted an extension until 29 November, stating that this deadline 'absolutely cannot be changed. After that, things are automatically going to happen'. Nomura could not know that the deadline coincided with the sailing of the Southern Operation task force. War was his shadow, gaining substance as the likelihood of peace waned.

Japanese naval vessels slipped out of anchorage in twos and threes to rendezvous at Tankan Bay in Etorofu (in the Kurile Islands) on 22 November 1941. They would sail on 26 November, following a northerly route to avoid accidental sightings by vessels and aircraft which operated on a more southerly route. They would meet oilers en route and refuel at 43°North, 170° East on 3 December 1941. Winter seas were rough, and little sea traffic strayed that far north of the equator; still, the accompanying forward destroyer screen had orders to sink any vessels, to keep their secret at any cost. Once underway, the fleet would maintain radio silence, and dummy transmissions from near the Japanese mainland would maintain the illusion for Allied listening posts that the task force was still in Japanese waters.

### The Hawaii Operation

The Japanese military plan had three phases. Phase one was to surprise Pearl Harbor, neutralize the American fleet and extend the perimeter to include Wake Island, the Gilberts, the northern Solomons, most of New

Pearl City

EAST LOCH

MIDDLE LOCH

65 aircraft in total stationed here, including PBYs, OS2Us, SU3s, J2Fs & SOC-1s

Mokunui Island

Mokuiki Island

Aircraft Hangars (for utility planes)

Aircraft Parking Area

Ford Island

Pearl Harbour NAS

Oil Storage Tanks

Dredge

Seaplane Ramps

Runway

Control Tower

Gasoline Wharf

Waipio Peninsula

Water Tower

Seaplane & Patrol Hangars

Seaplane Ramps

Dredge

Kuahua

Tower

US Naval Reservation

Floating Drydock

Hospital Point

Ten Ten Pier

Crane

Hammer-head Crane

SOUTH-EAST LOCH

Merry's Point

Drydock No 3
Drydock No2
Drydock No 1

Water Towers

District HQ

WEST LOCH

Naval Hospital

Oil Storage Tanks

Navy Yard

Waipio Point

N

Hale Makai Barracks

Aircraft Parking Strip

Hickam Air Force Base

0     500 yds

0     500 m

Bishop Point

Hawaiian Air Depot Hangars

= ship's number    YMS = minesweeper
date commissioned    PT = motor torpedo boats
. = date converted    AD = destroyer tender
= battleship    AV = seaplane tender
= destroyer    AH = hospital ship
= heavy cruiser    AK = cargo ship
= light cruiser    AO = oil tanker
= submarine    AR = repair ship
= minelayer    AX = auxiliary ship
= light minelayer    PG = patrol gunboat
= fast minesweeper

Guinea (a threat to Australia), Java, Sumatra, Malaya, Burma (east to the Indian border), Thailand, the Philippines and Borneo. Phase two was to strengthen military presence of the new perimeter. Phase three was defensive: to protect the perimeter and destroy any outside incursions.

Simultaneous army and navy attacks were to batter Pearl Harbor, the Philippines and Malaya. The army would land on the latter two and thrust towards Java. Wake Island, Thailand, Guam and Hong Kong would be occupied by the army. Two destroyers, *Ushio* and *Sazanami*, would shell Midway, and carriers returning from Pearl Harbor would complete the reduction of any defenders on Wake. Although there was no overall commander, army and navy attacks would be simultaneous: one swift thrust and the ripe fruits of the Pacific would fall into Japanese hands.

### Preparations

The plan called for a concentrated assault using dive-bombers, high altitude bombing and torpedo attacks. Bombers began practice runs, both high altitude and dive-bombing. The pilots' scores constantly improved and their hit ratios soared. Torpedo bombers began practicing, but their scores were less impressive, and although Genda did everything within his power, there was a barrier his men could not break, no matter how much they practiced. The harbor was too shallow for the conventional torpedoes then in use.

The US knew of the successful British torpedo attack at Taranto but they did not put out torpedo nets in Pearl Harbor: they were extremely time-consuming to erect and it was generally accepted that the harbor was too shallow for conventional torpedoes to function. This false sense of security was heightened by Pearl's seemingly impregnable defenses, which rendered sea bombardment an unlikely eventuality.

Japan identified bombing and torpedo runs as the most effective way to destroy the ships of the US fleet, based on British success at Taranto. The major problem however was that Japanese Model II torpedoes penetrated too deep in the water, and thus would stick in the shallow mud of the harbor.

Fuchida, Genda and Murata insisted that torpedo attacks improve to ten meters depth. Generally the attackers dropped torpedoes which hit the water, sank, and followed a depth of approximately 20m (65ft). With practice the pilots improved, but they could not achieve the ten meter requirement. Almost despairing, they studied the situation, and eventually devised an innovative solution; the use of torpedoes with added wooden fins. These would give them additional stability and provide enough extra buoyancy to successfully strike targets in shallow waters. The torpedoes sank to only 12m on average, but they operated on a straight and narrow course – a double improvement. Once they began fitting wooden fins and practicing with them, scores for kills in maneuvers rose dramatically to 70 per cent, and better on stationary vessels. (In 1944, after two years of torpedo pilot losses, scores were barely 15–18 per cent.)

Yamamoto now had torpedoes which would function in shallow Pearl Harbor, and although delivery was nearly the end of November, they had overcome their major hurdle. Following a concerted effort, the torpedoes were functioning satisfactorily by mid-November, and delivery by

*Akagi* launched all her aircraft against Pearl Harbor. Here Zero number AI-108 takes off. Each aircraft had a distinctive ID showing its carrier of origin: AI, *Akagi*; AII, *Kaga*; EI, *Shokaku*; EII, *Zuikaku*; BI, *Soryu*; and BII, *Hiryu*.

sailing was guaranteed. The plan for a torpedo attack thus moved from theory to reality.

Initially at ten per cent, Japanese bombing scores rose steadily to 80 per cent when both pilot and bombardier were made responsible for scoring a hit. (By 1944 pilot attrition had dropped bombing scores to 11 per cent.)

For identification purposes the Japanese had broken Pearl Harbor into district areas: A (between Ford Island and the Navy Yard); B (the north-west area of Ford Island); C (East Loch); D (Middle Loch); and E (West Loch). District A was subdivided into five areas: the docks north-west of the Navy Yard; the area mooring pillars; the area Navy Yard repair dock; the docks; and the remaining area. On a target constructed to resemble Pearl Harbor, they practiced their attack runs.

As of 3 December the Japanese knew *Oklahoma, Nevada, Enterprise,* two heavy cruisers and 12 destroyers had left Pearl Harbor, and five battleships, three heavy cruisers, three light cruisers, 12 destroyers and a seaplane tender had arrived. There seemed to be no unusual activity to suggest that the US was preparing for an attack, and shore leaves were granted as usual. On 4 December the disposition of ships was the same, and no undue air traffic was noted. As of 5 December *Oklahoma* and *Nevada* arrived in the harbor and *Lexington* and five cruisers departed: the total ships reported in harbor were eight battleships, three light cruisers, 16 destroyers and four *Honolulu* class light cruisers, as well as five destroyers. Also *Utah* and a seaplane tender re-entered the harbor. Furthermore, the report showed that no balloons were up, no blackout was enforced, no anti-torpedo nets had been deployed and there were no evident patrol flights. *Enterprise* was at sea on maneuvers. Life at Pearl Harbor followed a leisurely pace, as if there was no inkling of a Japanese attack.

Each part of the Pearl Harbor task force had responsibility for specific areas and targets: Air Attack Force (the carriers *Akagi, Kaga, Hiryu, Soryu, Shokaku* and *Zuikaku*), 1st Air Fleet, air attacks; 1st Destroyer Squadron (17th Destroyer Division, *Nagara* flagship and 18th Destroyer Division, *Akiguma,* flagship), screening and escort; 3rd Battleship Division (3rd BB Division and 8th Cruiser Division), screening and support; 2nd Submarine Division (*I-17* flagship, *I-21* and *I-23*), patrol; 7th Destroyer Division, the attack on Midway air base; 1st Supply Unit (*Kyokuto Maru* flagship, *Kenyo Maru, Kyokuto Maru, Kokuyo Maru* and *Shinkoku Maru*), supply; and 2nd Supply Unit (*Tohu Maru* supervisor, *Toei Maru, Shiriya,* and *Nippon Maru*), supply.

## 'Climb Mount Niitaka'

The Pearl Harbor task force sailed on 26 November towards Pearl Harbor, transmitters silent, radio operators listening while maintaining radio silence. Yamamoto sent Nagumo a coded message: '*Niitaka yama nobore*' ('Climb Mount Niitaka') meaning that the attacks would go forward as planned. Adm. Nagumo received a telegram on 2 December 1941 at 1700 hrs which told him to open a top secret envelope. Inside he found the fateful message: 'Our Empire has decided to go to war against the United States, Britain and Holland in early December.' The message set the date for 8 December (7 December, Pearl Harbor time). Nagumo told his officers the attack was on.

As the task force cruised onwards, the rolling winter seas encountered seemed to symbolize the world-wide turbulence heralded

**A composite pre-war photo showing aircraft superimposed above USS *Enterprise* in October 1941. On 7 December *Enterprise* was 180 miles south-south-west of Oahu, heading home after delivering aircraft to Wake Island.**

by these events. For the next five days the Japanese waited for an amendment, worried about a retraction of orders or an encounter which might tip their hand; but none came.

The day of 7 December arrived without reprieve. In Washington Nomura was told to expect a 14-part message which had to be translated and delivered to Hull by 1300 hrs Washington time. With difficulty he translated the document, but the 14-part message was incomplete, so he postponed the meeting with Hull for an hour. When all was translated except for the last part, Nomura headed for Hull's office. The time was 1420 hrs.

Despite Nomura's futile attempts to discover the reason for Tokyo's deadline, the designated hour passed without apparent action. US government code-breakers were still working on the message. Just after 0800 hrs Hawaiian time, Washington received the first reports from Pearl Harbor that they were under attack, and the terrible reality struck the code-breakers, who rushed to get copies to Marshall, Hull and others – but it was too late.

An awful sense of national helplessness, resulting in rage and determination, spread with the news reports. Suddenly, sharply, and with the jangling of an unwelcome alarm clock, Yamamoto's sleeping giant had awakened.

FIRST LIGHT AND THE FIRST WAVE DEPARTS; 0600 HRS, 7 DECEMBER
**The Zero fighters were the first planes to take off from the Japanese carriers, and they circled overhead, waiting for the Kates and Vals of the first attack wave to join them. On board *Akagi*, the Japanese command carrier, Cmdr Mitsuo Fuchida (observer, accompanied by Lt. Mitsuo Matazaki, pilot, and NAP 1/C Norinobu Mizuki) prepared to take off in Kate tail no. AI-301. Fuchida tied a *hachimaki* around his head, with the legend 'Certain Victory' on it. The ship's crew had been allowed special leave from their duties to witness this historic moment. There was no more delay: the hours of destiny for the Hawaii Operation lay directly ahead.**

# THE FIRST WAVE

In Pearl Harbor many shallow-draft vessels, such as this US Navy destroyer, refitted or took on stores from dockside directly, making the ships and dockside structures two-for-one targets for aircraft. Larger vessels had lighters and launches bring supplies aboard, and rubbish scows off-loaded their litter.

**N**ight darkened the sky and ocean, with only a faint demarcation between: true dawn was over an hour away. The minesweepers USS *Crossbill* and USS *Condor* patrolled 1.75 miles south of the Pearl Harbor entrance buoys. On watch aboard the *Condor* at 0342 hrs Ens. R.C. McCloy sighted a white wake and asked Quartermaster Uttrick what he thought the object was. Through glasses Uttrick identified it as a periscope, and at 0357 hrs contacted USS *Ward* on entrance patrol to investigate. Uttrick's blinker message read: 'Sighted submerged submarine on westerly course, speed nine knots.'

Lt. William Outerbridge commanded *Ward* while she patrolled the harbor entrance. A new officer on his first command, he was aware of degenerating relations between the US and Japan, and decided that what Uttrick had seen was most likely a Japanese submarine. He requested a status report from *Condor* and was told that their last sighting was at 0350 hrs and that the object was moving towards the harbor entrance. 'Sound general quarters', Outerbridge ordered.

For the next hour the USS *Ward* conducted a fruitless sonar sweep of the area. At 0435 hrs Outerbridge had *Ward* stepped down from general quarters. The protective net to Pearl Harbor was scheduled to swing open at 0458 hrs to admit the minelayers, and would remain open until 0840 hrs. Although they did not know it, the sub probably intended to shadow the minesweeper into the safety of the harbor, a wolf sliding in among the sheep.

A sighting, although not an everyday occurrence, was not unheard of, and was logged. *Ward* continued her rounds. Entering the harbor after a standard tour of duty at 0458 hrs, *Crossbill* and *Condor* returned to their berths. The harbor's anti-submarine net did not close.

*Pennsylvania* bore a catapult on her X-turret. Like many battleships at Pearl, she often spread a canvas over the deck to give crewmen some relief from the sun and heat.

A single-observation seaplane, JI-1, one of five, catapulted from the cruiser *Tone* at 0530 hrs. Seconds later JII-1 from *Chikuma* joined it. Together they winged through the dawn towards Lahaina and Pearl Harbor anchorages respectively; their orders – survey target areas and report on the conditions, breaking radio silence. Their mission was literally the last chance for the Japanese Navy to abort the planned attack, shoud it be deemed necessary.

The sun rose on a fair Sunday, with mainly high clouds, and a sea whose swells were increasing. At 0530 hrs, the Japanese task force swung to port, heading into a 14-knot wind. The carriers increased their speed to 24 knots. They pitched 12–15° in the increasing swells; but the decision had been made, and *Akagi* signaled the aircraft of the first wave to prepare for take-off.

South of Pearl Harbor at 0600 hrs, 18 SBDs took off from the USS *Enterprise* on a routine scouting mission to fly ahead and land at Ford Island, according to Halsey's instructions. Although aware of uneasy Japanese–US relations, this seemed a routine training mission and they planned to arrive in time for breakfast, around 0800 hrs. The *Enterprise* lay 200 miles south of Oahu and was heading home. Cmdr H.L. Young piloted one SBD; Lt.Cmdr Nichol, Halsey's flag secretary, flew with him.

Nearly 220 miles north of Oahu, the first planes steadily took off from the six Japanese carriers and circled, waiting for all 183 of the aircraft in the first wave to join them. Two aircraft were lost during take-off. At 0610 hrs they took up V-formation, like homing geese, and headed south-south-east towards their primary target, Pearl Harbor naval basin. Cmdr Fuchida noted such pristine beauty in the early morning that he vividly recalled the scene decades later.

The crew of the USS *Antares*, a supply ship, sighted what they thought was a sub and notified *Ward* at 0630 hrs. As an ASW precaution, a PBY was launched from Oahu. When *Ward* arrived on the scene, Lt. Outerbridge saw what appeared to be a submarine's conning tower breaking the surface. Though it could have been friendly, the vessel did not surface or attempt to communicate. Following standing orders that

**Many minesweepers patrolled the waters off the Hawaiian chain. At the beginning of World War II many coastal minesweepers were converted trawlers or members of the *Bird* class.**

unidentified vessels were considered hostile, Outerbridge opened fire at 0645 hrs. One round penetrated the sub's conning tower. The PBY circled, seeing the confrontation, and joined the attack. *Ward* covered the projected course of the unknown submarine with depth charges. Without knowing it, the Americans had fired the first shots in the battle for Pearl Harbor.

The sub did not resurface, and Outerbridge thought they had hit her. At 0653 hrs he sent coded signals to 14th Naval District headquarters, saying: 'Attacked, fired upon, and dropped depth charges upon a submarine operating in a defensive area.' At 0706 hrs Outerbridge dropped more depth charges and saw a black oil slick forming on the surface.

Excerpt from a Japanese newsreel, showing a Kate taking off from a carrier. In Hawaii Operation the carriers turned into the wind to launch the aircraft that attacked Pearl Harbor and US military installations.

Hawaiian radio stations often broadcast music all night when flights of incoming aircraft were expected from the mainland United States. This was one such night. The station's signal was loud and clear to the approaching Japanese, and at 0700 hrs Cmdr Fuchida ordered his men to use it as a directional locator. Less than five minutes later privates Lockhard and Elliott, manning the mobile US Army radar post at Opana, saw a blip on their screen, a sizable force of unidentified aircraft, 132 miles north of Oahu and closing. They wondered where the aircraft were from and if the radar station's equipment was defective. If the blip was accurate, its size indicated a group of more than 50 aircraft.

At 0710 hrs Elliott notified headquarters at Ft Shafter but failed to mention the blip's size. The duty officer, Lt. Tyler, had been assigned to Ft Shafter less than a week and knew of no incoming flights from the north, and so for ten minutes they discussed the blip and its possible implications. By this time the blip was 72 miles north and closing.

At 0715 hrs the duty officers of the 14th Naval District and Adm. Kimmel received Outerbridge's message which had been delayed in decoding. About 220 miles north the second wave of the Japanese attack – 168 aircraft – took off.

Lt. Tyler decided that the blip Elliott had reported was probably B-17s scheduled to arrive from the mainland. He told the privates things were OK and instructed them to shut down the radar station. Uneasy, Lockhard and Eliott continued to monitor the blip's approach, despite Tyler's instructions. The time was 0720 hrs.

At 0730 hrs Washington time, Kramer received the final installment of the Japanese 14-part message. It read: 'The Japanese Government regrets … it is impossible to reach an agreement through further negotiations.' The message was assembled and sent to Adm. Stark, and when taken to Stark, someone commented: 'the virulence and tenor of the language … was enough to indicate that we could expect war'. Wilkinson suggested sending an additional warning to Pearl Harbor, but the officers decided to do nothing at that time.

Bratton assembled the entire message and read it, trying to work out its significance. While he was doing so, a shorter intercept arrived from Togo to Ambassador Nomura. This stated: 'Will the Ambassador please submit to the United States Government … our reply at 1:00pm. on the

Old Pali Pass lookout in the Koolau Range overlooks Kaneohe and was a landmark for Japanese fliers. Changed in the 1950s, the road no longer exists in this fashion.

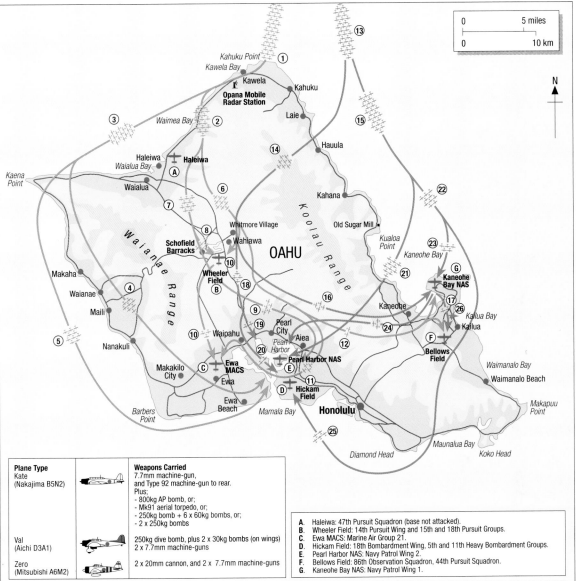

| Plane Type | | Weapons Carried |
|---|---|---|
| Kate (Nakajima B5N2) | | 7.7mm machine-gun, and Type 92 machine-gun to rear. Plus; - 800kg AP bomb, or; - Mk91 aerial torpedo, or; - 250kg bomb + 6 x 60kg bombs, or; - 2 x 250kg bombs |
| Val (Aichi D3A1) | | 250kg dive bomb, plus 2 x 30kg bombs (on wings) 2 x 7.7mm machine-guns |
| Zero (Mitsubishi A6M2) | | 2 x 20mm cannon, and 2 x 7.7mm machine-guns |

A. Haleiwa: 47th Pursuit Squadron (base not attacked).
B. Wheeler Field: 14th Pursuit Wing and 15th and 18th Pursuit Groups.
C. Ewa MACS: Marine Air Group 21.
D. Hickam Field: 18th Bombardment Wing, 5th and 11th Heavy Bombardment Groups.
E. Pearl Harbor NAS: Navy Patrol Wing 2.
F. Bellows Field: 86th Observation Squadron, 44th Pursuit Squadron.
G. Kaneohe Bay NAS: Navy Patrol Wing 1.

### Wave 1

1. The First Attack Wave (total 183 aircraft) splits into two as it crosses over Kahuku Point at approximately 0735 hrs.
2. 2nd and 3rd Attack Groups (total 94 aircraft) split off from the main wave.
3. First Attack Group (led by Lt.Com. Fuchida consisting of 89 Kates) heads South West, skirting over the Southern edge of Oahu. Their intended target is Ford Island and Battleship Row.
4. 1st, 2nd, 3rd and 4th Torpedo Attack Units split off; Lt.Com. Shigeharu Murata is in charge. Total aircraft, 40 Kates armed with Mk 91 torpedoes: intended targets, the key battleships on either side of Ford Island.
5. 1st, 2nd, 3rd, and 4th Attack Units (led by Fuchida) split off and head for Battleship Row from deeper south. Their aim is to approach from the South, over Barber's Point, to disguise their attack path and avoid detection over land. Total aircraft 49 Kates, armed with 800kg bombs.
6. 3rd Attack Group (1st, 2nd, 3rd, 4th, 5th, and 6th Fighter Combat Units: total 43 Zeros) heads for the US air bases on Oahu, for strafing runs.
7. 2nd Attack Group comprising 15th and 16th Attack Units (51 Val dive-bombers, armed with 250kg bombs) heads for Wheeler Field, Schofield Barracks, Hickam and Pearl Harbor NAS.
8. 16th Attack Unit under Lt. Sakamoto (25 Vals) hits Wheeler Field air base.
9. 15th Attack Unit under Lt.Com. Takahashi (26 Vals) heads for Hickam Field and Pearl Harbor NAS.
10. 3rd and 4th Fighter Combat Units (14 Zeros) strafe Wheeler Field and EWA air bases.
11. 1st and 2nd Fighter Combat Units (under Lt.Com. Itaya, total 18 Zeros) hit Hickam Field and then EWA.
12. 5th and 6th Fighter Units (Lt. Kaneko, total 11 Zeros) strafe Kaneohe NAS and Bellows field.

### Wave 2

13. 0840 hrs, on reaching Oahu the Japanese 2nd Attack Wave (total 168 planes, under the command of Lt.Com. Shigekazu Shimazaki) splits into two.
14. 3rd Attack Group (36 Zero fighters, under Lt. Shindo) heads for strafing attacks on the US air bases.
15. 1st and 2nd Attack Groups (78 Val dive-bombers and 54 Kates, under Lt.Com. Shigekazu) head for Battleship Row and the air bases.
16. 3rd and 4th Fighter Units (18 Zeros, under Lt. Iida) head for Kaneohe NAS and Bellows Field.
17. 4th Fighter Unit (9 Zeros under Lt. Nono) hits Bellows Field air base.
18. 1st and 2nd Fighter Units (18 Zeros, under Lt. Shindo) head for Pearl Harbor NAS and Hickam Field.
19. 2nd Fighter Unit (under Lt. Nikaido, 9 Zeros) hits Pearl Harbor NAS on Ford Island.
20. 1st Fighter Unit (9 Zeros, under Lt. Shindo) hits Hickam Field air base.
21. 2nd Attack Group (78 Vals dive-bombers, under Lt.Com. Takashige Egusa) splits off, and heads for Battleship Row, Ford Island and the Navy Yard at Pearl Harbor (to pick up any missed targets from the first wave).
22. 1st Attack Group (54 Kates, under Lt.Com. Shigekazu Shimazaki) heads for Kaneohe, Hickam and Pearl Harbor NAS air bases.
23. 3rd Attack Unit (27 Kates under Lt. Tatsuo Ichihara) hits Kaneohe NAS.
24. 5th Attack Unit proceeds to bomb Pearl Harbor NAS on Ford Island.
25. 6th Attack Unit (27 Kates under Lt.Com. Shimazaki) hits Hickam Field.
26. Nono's 4th Fighter Unit encounters six fighters from the 47th Pursuit Squadron: a dog-fight ensues, and seven Japanese planes are shot down.

ABOVE **A 1940 US Army field communications unit. Such a unit was near Opana, where the approaching Japanese aircraft were first noticed; but they were later dismissed as incoming B-17s.**

7th, your time.' Bratton tried to reach Marshall but was unable to do so until 1030 hrs Washington time. Kramer almost casually noted that with the time differential involved, it would be 0730 hrs Pearl Harbor time.

Gen. Marshall's telegram to Short arrived at RCA in Honolulu but was not identified as a priority message and was given to RCA Messenger Tadao Fuchikami at 0733 hrs. He was to deliver it to Short's HQ in the normal course of his morning rounds.

At 0738 hrs a recon 'Jake' from *Chikuma* gave a visual confirmation that the main US fleet was in Pearl Harbor: 'Enemy ... at anchor, nine battleships, one heavy cruiser, six light cruisers.' The pilot related conditions important to the approaching first wave: 'Wind direction from 80°, speed 14m, clearance over enemy fleet 1,700m, cloud density seven.' The recon aircraft from *Tone* reported: 'Enemy ... not in Lahaina anchorage.' Although brief, the message had tremendous overtones, because all hopes and plans for catching the Americans at the deep-water Lahaina anchorage (off Maui Island, 80 miles south-east of Oahu) were dashed, and confirmed that the attack would concentrate on the shallow Pearl Harbor anchorage. Their new torpedo modifications would get their baptism of fire. Having reported, the pilot swept wide to the south, trying to find the carriers; but he did not fly far enough, and *Enterprise* remained undiscovered.

By 0739 hrs at Opana Eliott and Lockhard had lost the incoming blip because of the radar blind zone caused by the hills between Opana and the Japanese attack force. A minute later Fuchida dropped below the clouds and sighted the northern shore beneath Oahu's empty skies:

The Japanese first wave had the sky to themselves. Fuchida remembered many years later how peaceful and quiet it had appeared when his pilot dropped his plane below the clouds and he first saw Oahu.

no enemy aircraft. Fuchida felt relieved that the attack was going according to plan, a quick surprise thrust.

At 0749 hrs Fuchida ordered his pilots to deploy into attack formation by firing a single shot from his flare gun, signifying 'torpedo planes to attack'. His radioman tapped out the signal 'To-To-To' (the first syllable of *tosugekiseyo*, meaning 'to charge'). Then Fuchida thought Suganami may have missed his signal and fired a second shot. Takahashi saw both shots and misunderstood, thinking dive-bombers were to strike: he ordered his dive-bombers into immediate attacks. Murata observed both shots and then saw Takahashi's plane (EI-238) gliding into attack formation. He knew there had been a misunderstanding, but it could not be rectified, so he led his torpedo group into its attack pattern.

Torpedo forces split into two groups of eight planes each, one under Matsumura and one under Nagai, and closed on their targets in the West Loch. Groups of 12 torpedo bombers, under Kitajima flying AII-311 and Murata piloting AI-311, angled over Hickam and then down Battleship Row. Aircraft dived in formations of two or three planes, each singling out its designated target. If a target was questionable, pilots and bombardiers were ordered to make passes until they had reasonable certainty of a hit. If they could not acquire their target, they could then elect to strike another.

At 0753 hrs Fuchida radioed the task force on a broad band: '*Tora, Tora, Tora*' ('Tiger, Tiger, Tiger'), indicating that so far their approach had been a complete success and the US naval and army installations had been caught unaware.

At 0748 hrs Kaneohe came under attack; at 0800 hrs bombs began falling on Wheeler Field, eight miles from Pearl Harbor. When the Japanese attacked Kaneohe, the OD notified Bellows Field, who thought he was making them the butt of a practical joke – until the Japanese hit Bellows too. Japanese first-wave attack aircraft descended on Ford Island,

LEFT **Diamond Head, seen from the north, with Honolulu in the foreground. Many Japanese pilots used it a distinctive landmark during their approach for the attack on Pearl Harbor.**

**41**

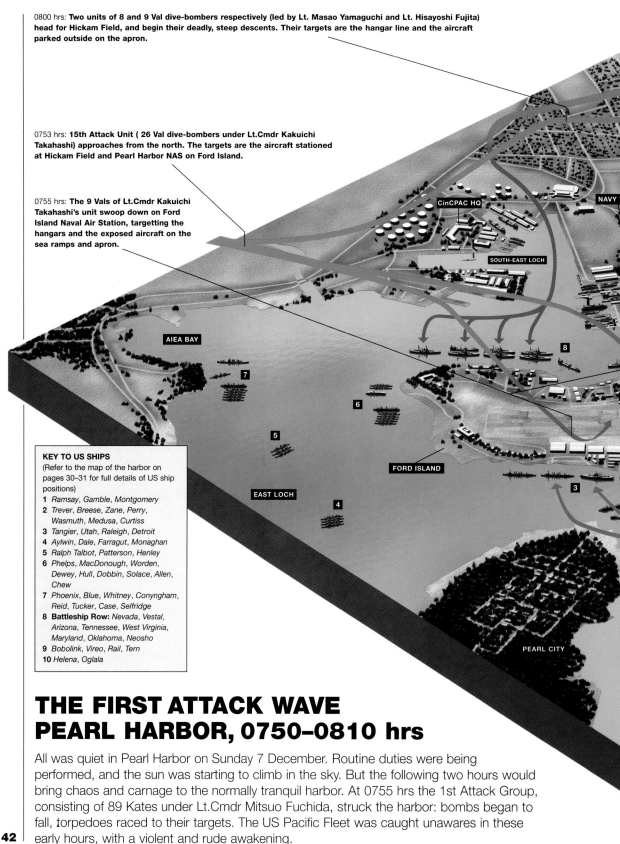

**0800 hrs:** Two units of 8 and 9 Val dive-bombers respectively (led by Lt. Masao Yamaguchi and Lt. Hisayoshi Fujita) head for Hickam Field, and begin their deadly, steep descents. Their targets are the hangar line and the aircraft parked outside on the apron.

**0753 hrs:** 15th Attack Unit ( 26 Val dive-bombers under Lt.Cmdr Kakuichi Takahashi) approaches from the north. The targets are the aircraft stationed at Hickam Field and Pearl Harbor NAS on Ford Island.

**0755 hrs:** The 9 Vals of Lt.Cmdr Kakuichi Takahashi's unit swoop down on Ford Island Naval Air Station, targetting the hangars and the exposed aircraft on the sea ramps and apron.

CinCPAC HQ

NAVY Y

SOUTH-EAST LOCH

AIEA BAY

**7**

**6**

**5**

**8**

FORD ISLAND

**3**

EAST LOCH

**4**

PEARL CITY

**KEY TO US SHIPS**
(Refer to the map of the harbor on pages 30–31 for full details of US ship positions)
**1** *Ramsay, Gamble, Montgomery*
**2** *Trever, Breese, Zane, Perry,*
 *Wasmuth, Medusa, Curtiss*
**3** *Tangier, Utah, Raleigh, Detroit*
**4** *Aylwin, Dale, Farragut, Monaghan*
**5** *Ralph Talbot, Patterson, Henley*
**6** *Phelps, MacDonough, Worden,*
 *Dewey, Hull, Dobbin, Solace, Allen,*
 *Chew*
**7** *Phoenix, Blue, Whitney, Conyngham,*
 *Reid, Tucker, Case, Selfridge*
**8** **Battleship Row:** *Nevada, Vestal,*
 *Arizona, Tennessee, West Virginia,*
 *Maryland, Oklahoma, Neosho*
**9** *Bobolink, Vireo, Rail, Tern*
**10** *Helena, Oglala*

# THE FIRST ATTACK WAVE
# PEARL HARBOR, 0750–0810 hrs

All was quiet in Pearl Harbor on Sunday 7 December. Routine duties were being performed, and the sun was starting to climb in the sky. But the following two hours would bring chaos and carnage to the normally tranquil harbor. At 0755 hrs the 1st Attack Group, consisting of 89 Kates under Lt.Cmdr Mitsuo Fuchida, struck the harbor: bombs began to fall, torpedoes raced to their targets. The US Pacific Fleet was caught unawares in these early hours, with a violent and rude awakening.

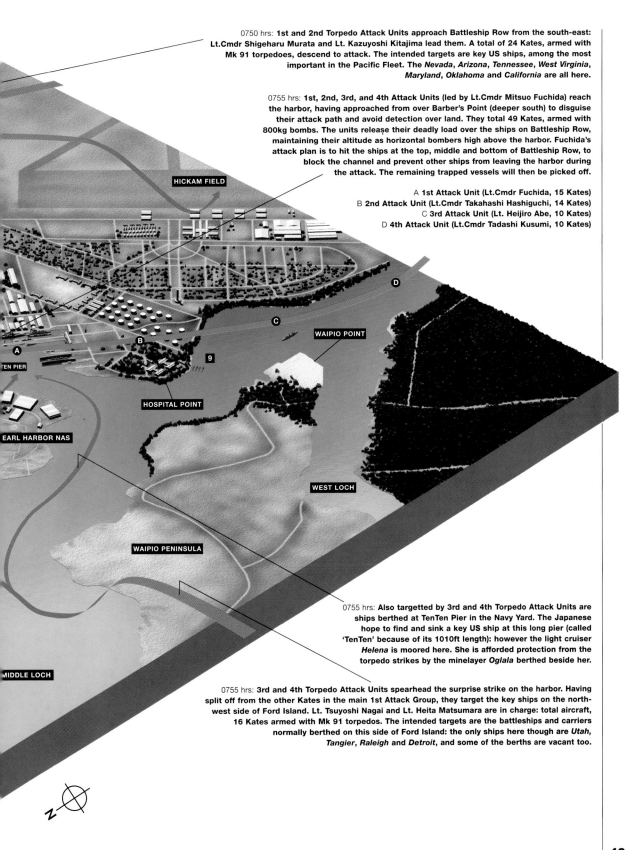

**0750 hrs: 1st and 2nd Torpedo Attack Units approach Battleship Row from the south-east:** Lt.Cmdr Shigeharu Murata and Lt. Kazuyoshi Kitajima lead them. A total of 24 Kates, armed with Mk 91 torpedoes, descend to attack. The intended targets are key US ships, among the most important in the Pacific Fleet. The *Nevada*, *Arizona*, *Tennessee*, *West Virginia*, *Maryland*, *Oklahoma* and *California* are all here.

**0755 hrs: 1st, 2nd, 3rd, and 4th Attack Units (led by Lt.Cmdr Mitsuo Fuchida) reach** the harbor, having approached from over Barber's Point (deeper south) to disguise their attack path and avoid detection over land. They total 49 Kates, armed with 800kg bombs. The units release their deadly load over the ships on Battleship Row, maintaining their altitude as horizontal bombers high above the harbor. Fuchida's attack plan is to hit the ships at the top, middle and bottom of Battleship Row, to block the channel and prevent other ships from leaving the harbor during the attack. The remaining trapped vessels will then be picked off.

A **1st Attack Unit (Lt.Cmdr Fuchida, 15 Kates)**
B **2nd Attack Unit (Lt.Cmdr Takahashi Hashiguchi, 14 Kates)**
C **3rd Attack Unit (Lt. Heijiro Abe, 10 Kates)**
D **4th Attack Unit (Lt.Cmdr Tadashi Kusumi, 10 Kates)**

HICKAM FIELD

D

C

WAIPIO POINT

A

B

9

TEN PIER

HOSPITAL POINT

EARL HARBOR NAS

WEST LOCH

WAIPIO PENINSULA

**0755 hrs: Also targetted by 3rd and 4th Torpedo Attack Units are** ships berthed at TenTen Pier in the Navy Yard. The Japanese hope to find and sink a key US ship at this long pier (called 'TenTen' because of its 1010ft length): however the light cruiser *Helena* is moored here. She is afforded protection from the torpedo strikes by the minelayer *Oglala* berthed beside her.

MIDDLE LOCH

**0755 hrs: 3rd and 4th Torpedo Attack Units spearhead the surprise strike on the harbor. Having** split off from the other Kates in the main 1st Attack Group, they target the key ships on the north-west side of Ford Island. Lt. Tsuyoshi Nagai and Lt. Heita Matsumara are in charge: total aircraft, 16 Kates armed with Mk 91 torpedos. The intended targets are the battleships and carriers normally berthed on this side of Ford Island: the only ships here though are *Utah*, *Tangier*, *Raleigh* and *Detroit*, and some of the berths are vacant too.

N

Hickam, Bellows and Ewa airfields. Torpedo bombers began their runs on Battleship Row. Pearl Harbor was under attack.

When Cmdr Harold M. Martin reached Kaneohe it was too late. The 36 PBYs under his command were sitting ducks. The anti-aircraft batteries which should have been there had been returned to army bases on the Friday afternoon. Four PBYs were moored less than 1,000 yards apart, and four more were inside Hangar 1. Zeros struck first, gliding down low and strafing, bullets chewing up tarmac and ripping through planes. The field's fire truck was also destroyed. Martin had not yet reached his headquarters when the first PBY in the water was ablaze.

On this particular Sunday morning all was SOP – business as usual – in the Pacific Fleet. Chapel services were planned, mess halls and galleys

were laying out breakfast, launches to and from shore were readying, and men on duty rosters were preparing for their watch. Japanese aircraft swooped out of the morning sky, lining their sights on capital ships.

At 0755 hrs Lt.Cmdr Logan Ramsey stood at the Ford Island Command Center watching the color guard hoist the flag. A plane buzzed them and he snapped, 'Get that fellow's number!' He studied the area, noting: 'I saw something … fall out of that plane …' An explosion from the hangar area cut his words short. Racing across the way, Ramsey ordered the radioman to send out the following message: 'Air raid, Pearl Harbor. This is NO drill.' The clock read 0758 hrs.

In a moment the scene of battleships and tenders preparing for morning services, mess call and watch changes was transformed to battle alert. Torpedo planes nosed down, leveling and dropping their deadly loads into the water. Wakes streaked towards berthed vessels. Observers were confused, surprised and horrified as the nature of the situation dawned. R.Adm. W.R. Furlong aboard the *Oglala*, which was berthed in the *Pennsylvania*'s normal position, saw a bomb fall from one of the approaching aircraft. He made a mental note that the flyer would be in trouble with his CO, when the plane banked and Furlong saw its insignia – a Rising Sun! 'Japanese!' He yelled: 'Man your stations!'

Ensign R.S. Brooks aboard *West Virginia* saw what he erroneously thought was a shipboard explosion on *California*. Reacting instantly, he ordered hands to turn to for an Away Fire and Rescue Party. Men boiled up from bunks to help.

Matasumura and Nagai's formations sped like arrows to the target. West of Ford Island, *Utah* and *Raleigh* reeled under torpedo explosions. On Battleship Row, Goto flew straight at *Oklahoma*, released his torpedo and climbed. 'It hit!' Cried his observer as a huge jet of water geysered upward.

Aboard *Raleigh* confusion reigned. At 0755 hrs a torpedo knocked out electrical power before anyone could sound battle stations. Sailors immediately manned *Raleigh*'s 3-in. guns, which had ammo in ready boxes, while she began listing to port. East of Ford Island, TenTen Pier

The *Arizona* was the worst hit. Slammed by bombs, she quickly sank, taking over 1,200 seamen down with her. Half the US casualties at Pearl Harbor were on this one vessel.

BELOW On Ford Island NAS, Kingfishers, Catalinas and other naval aircraft were savaged. In the background smoke rises from the damaged battleship *Nevada*, while the bright plume of smoke billows skyward as Shaw explodes.

experienced the first slashing attack. The USS *Helena* shook as torpedoes bit into her starboard side. Nagai headed towards *Pennsylvania* but realized she was protected from torpedo attack and decided to loose his fish on *Oglala*, moored adjacent to *Helena*. *Oglala* was crippled in the attack and *Helena* rocked in the water.

Aboard the *Vestal* at 0755 hrs CWO Hall saw the bombers, identified them as Japanese and sounded general quarters. Men poured from below decks and the mess area, and within ten minutes *Vestal*'s guns were firing at the invaders. She took two hits, one to port and one to starboard, each killing a crewman. A torpedo loosed at them went deep and under their keel, much to their relief.

About 0800 hrs crewmen Huffman and de Jong of *PT 23*, a *Higgins* class 78-ton patrol torpedo boat, saw aircraft (identified as Japanese by the 'meatball' Rising Sun insignia on their wings) swooping in and dropping bombs and torpedoes. They argued about what the aircraft were doing, awakening Ensign Ed Farley, who had been sleeping below deck after a late night on the town. Farley made his way to the deck, wiping sleep from his eyes and yawning. Following their gaze, he was horrified to see one plane fly over them on dead course for *California*: an instant later the battleship was rocked by an explosion. Huffman and de Jong jumped into a gun turret and fired on the attacking aircraft with twin .50-cal. machine-guns. One attacking aircraft wobbled and then went down, possibly the first blood the American anti-aircraft fire had drawn.

Across the navy basin, on the shore opposite the sub base, *Ramapo* was in the process of loading six additional PT boats in cradles for transport to the Philippines. When the attack began, crews of the PT boats tried to man their guns, but the turrets would not move because the engines had

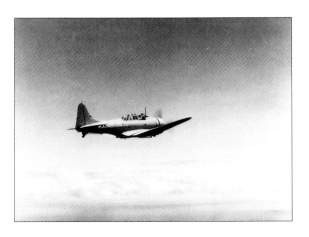

An SBD-2 Dauntless dive-bomber from USS *Enterprise* in pre-war colors. The legend in front of the body rondel identified the plane. These dive-bombers flew into the shooting match between vessels and attackers on the morning of Sunday 7 December.

been shut down for transport. No engines, no power, no movable turrets. Crewmen began rotating turrets by muscle-power, while gunners turned barrels red-hot with fire. Boats in cradles already on *Ramapo*'s deck felt especially vulnerable – neither on land nor in the water – as attackers blasted vessels and dived with guns chattering.

The USS *Arizona*'s band played while the flag was being raised just before 0800 hrs. They heard the dull and constant thudding of distant bombs; one or two nearby vessels seemed to have gone crazy, firing their guns. Suddenly *Vestal*, a repair ship moored outboard of *Arizona*, opened fire. The time was 0805 hrs. A torpedo dipped under *Vestal* and gutted the battleship, blowing 'the bottom out of *Arizona*'.

About 0805 hrs Cpt. Shoemaker, commander of Ford Island, gritted his teeth and stared at the seaplane apron and hangar which was blazing 'like a forest fire'. Only a few seaplanes were undamaged, and Shoemaker organized work crews to move undamaged ones away from those that were burning.

At 0810 hrs a bomb hit *Arizona* starboard of No. 4 turret and she convulsed. The bomb pierced her forward magazine, and the concussion was so powerful that damage control parties aboard nearby *Vestal* were blown overboard when a fireball erupted skyward from *Arizona*'s magazine. Immediately *Arizona* began settling. Until now, outboard vessels had suffered the majority of the torpedo damage, but as bombers arrived, inboard ships were targeted.

The USS *Oklahoma*, outboard of the *Maryland*, was staggered by torpedo hits. Men rushed to ammo lockers, only to find them secured. Once lockers had been forced open, there was no compressed air to power the guns, and the ship had begun to list markedly when a third torpedo knifed home. Rescue parties began pulling sailors from below decks, up shell hoists and to the deck while her executive officer, Cmdr J.L. Kenworthy, realized she was in danger of capsizing. He gave the order to abandon ship by the starboard side and to climb over the side onto the bottom as it rolled over. Nearby *California* quivered when a torpedo impacted.

In the harbor nearly 150 crewmen were on *Oklahoma*'s side when a fourth torpedo hit her. As one crewman said, *Oklahoma* 'bounced up and … settled down … turned over': the battleship slowly rolled until her barnacled bottom saw daylight. *Vestal* had fires blazing around her and seemed likely to catch fire. As *Oklahoma* capsized, *Arizona* was struck, and the explosion which followed knocked men off nearby vessels through the might of its concussion: a bomb struck near No. 2 turret, and exploded her forward magazine. Fires aboard *Vestal* were extinguished like someone blowing out a match when *Arizona*'s magazine exploded.

When fire-fighting crews tried to man the hoses, there was no water pressure. *Arizona* lay on the water mains. An alert ensign cut on the fire sprinkler system and wet down fuel storage tanks on the tank farm. Across from the tanks *Neosho*'s anti-aircraft batteries peppered the sky in front of incoming aircraft. After *Oklahoma*'s hit *Neosho* made preparations

US Army Air Corps B-17s were being flown in from the mainland. These uninformed and unarmed Flying Fortresses arrived in the middle of the Japanese attack. Two Vals are visible off the B-17's port wing.

to get underway. She was half-loaded with high octane aircraft fuel which she had been unloading just minutes before the first air strike: if hit, she would immolate nearby vessels, including *Maryland*, *Tennessee* and *West Virginia*. Slowly *Neosho*'s stacks fumed, and she moved away from anchorage.

Sirens blared. All across the harbor shipboard intercoms and PAs blasted out general quarters. Aircraft were ordered up to seek out the enemy. Sluggishly vessels began to respond, smoke pouring at first slowly and then steadily from their stacks and their sporadic anti-aircraft fire dotted the skies, filled with aircraft displaying the Rising Sun. One Val was hit, and crashed onto *Curtiss*' deck, but without doing great damage to the moving ship. The target ship *Utah* began to settle, turning over: a shuddering *Oklahoma* had capsized. Damage control parties aboard *Raleigh* fought to keep her afloat and upright while the first wisps of oily smoke from a score of vessels rose into the morning sky.

At 0800 hrs stripped-down, unarmed B-17s en route from the mainland United States (which Tyler thought were the unidentified radar blip) sighted Oahu and began their descent. Meanwhile the recon SBDs from the USS *Enterprise* commenced their approach to the airfield. Some were stitched by enemy aircraft, and hungry American anti-aircraft batteries also sought them out. Enemy and friendly aircraft mixed, while undiscriminating anti-aircraft fire reached to slap them all from the skies.

Adm. Kimmel observed the beginning of the attack from his home. He summoned his driver and rushed to headquarters. Cmdr Daubin of Sub Squadron Four went with him. Kimmel arrived at CinCPAC HQ and watched helplessly as plane after plane dived, wheeled and circled the now-smoking ships in the anchorage like vultures. He later said: 'My main thought was the fate of my ships.'

In the midst of the fighting one SBD from *Enterprise* landed. Young and Nichol deplaned on the pitted runway as anti-aircraft fire dotted the sky. 'They're shooting at my own boys,' Young yelled, pointing at his incoming recon group: 'Tell Kimmel.' American fire knocked one SBD into the sea, but its crew was rescued. Zeros shot down four. One SBD was hit and its crew bailed out near Ewa: another crash-landed at Kauai on Burns Field. The remainder reached Ford or Ewa later in the day: they would be refitted and sent hunting for the Japanese fleet.

Lt.Cmdr F.J. Thomas was the ranking officer aboard *Nevada* and Ensign J.K. Taussig Jr was officer of the deck and acting air defense officer when general quarters sounded. Taussig ran to the nearest gun. At 0802 hrs *Nevada* blasted a torpedo plane which was approaching its port beam beginning a torpedo run. *Nevada*'s five-inch guns and 50-cal. machine-guns poured fire into the aircraft. A second approaching torpedo plane was also hit, but managed to release its torpedo: silvery streaks sliced the water and threw up white wakes on an intersect course with *Nevada*. The explosion punched a hole in *Nevada*'s port bow: compartments flooded and she began to list to port. Japanese bombers dropped their payloads near her port quarter. Thomas ordered counter-flooding. Burning fuel oil from *Arizona* drifted towards *Nevada*, and Thomas ordered her underway to avoid it. Meanwhile Taussig was hit in the thigh and refused aid while he commanded a gun crew. Lt. Ruff came aboard from a launch. He suggested Thomas manage *Nevada*'s action from below decks and Ruff would manage them from above. Smoking and listing, *Nevada* struggled towards the harbor entrance.

South-west of *Arizona*, *California* rocked in the water as a second port-side torpedo struck home. Acting decisively, Ens. Edgar Fain ordered countermeasures to prevent capsizing. High above the harbor the drone of bombers closed. Then bombs began falling on Battleship Row from high above.

Cpt. Langdon's B-17s from the mainland were due to land at Hickam at any moment. Base commander Col. Farthing was in the control tower, waiting with Cpt. Blake, his operations officer, who was to guide in the aircraft. A swarm of planes topped the horizon from the north, flying low and fast. Some bypassed Hickam and flew towards Kaneohe and Ford Island, but nine bombers made a beeline for Hickam Field.

Lt.Col. James Mollison was at home when the attack began. He rushed outside and saw the planes make their initial passes; then he ran inside, dressed and went to headquarters. Once there he called Short's office in Oahu to report that they were under attack. To emphasize his point, he held the receiver so Phillips (Short's chief of staff) could hear the bombs falling.

Bombs splintered the repair hangar, a supply building, the base chapel, the enlisted men's club, guardhouse and the enlisted men's mess hall, where 35 men were killed as they ate breakfast. Cpt. B.E. Allen got his B-17 rolling down the runway, his one thought to take the fight to the skies. The Zeros seemed to single out the mighty B-17s, and 7.7mm bullets rent the Flying Fortresses where they were parked. Allen could not get all four engines to crank, so he taxied his aircraft away from the others which were being savaged.

Langdon's B-17s reached Hickam as the attack was getting into full swing. Manned by skeleton crews, unarmed and low on fuel after their

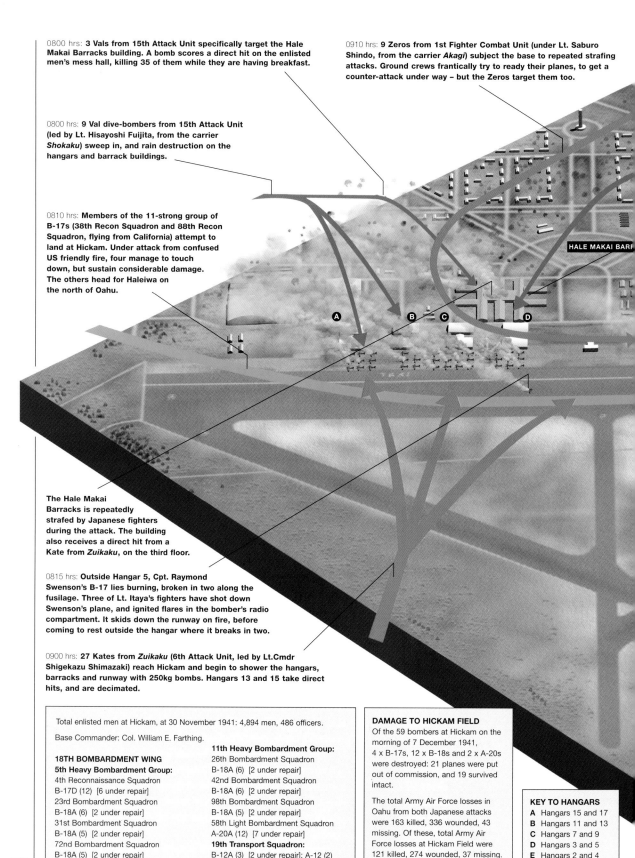

**0800 hrs: 3 Vals from 15th Attack Unit** specifically target the Hale Makai Barracks building. A bomb scores a direct hit on the enlisted men's mess hall, killing 35 of them while they are having breakfast.

**0910 hrs: 9 Zeros from 1st Fighter Combat Unit** (under Lt. Saburo Shindo, from the carrier *Akagi*) subject the base to repeated strafing attacks. Ground crews frantically try to ready their planes, to get a counter-attack under way – but the Zeros target them too.

**0800 hrs: 9 Val dive-bombers from 15th Attack Unit** (led by Lt. Hisayoshi Fuijita, from the carrier *Shokaku*) sweep in, and rain destruction on the hangars and barrack buildings.

**0810 hrs: Members of the 11-strong group of B-17s** (38th Recon Squadron and 88th Recon Squadron, flying from California) attempt to land at Hickam. Under attack from confused US friendly fire, four manage to touch down, but sustain considerable damage. The others head for Haleiwa on the north of Oahu.

HALE MAKAI BARR

Ⓐ Ⓑ Ⓒ Ⓓ

The Hale Makai Barracks is repeatedly strafed by Japanese fighters during the attack. The building also receives a direct hit from a Kate from *Zuikaku*, on the third floor.

**0815 hrs: Outside Hangar 5, Cpt. Raymond Swenson's B-17** lies burning, broken in two along the fuselage. Three of Lt. Itaya's fighters have shot down Swenson's plane, and ignited flares in the bomber's radio compartment. It skids down the runway on fire, before coming to rest outside the hangar where it breaks in two.

**0900 hrs: 27 Kates from *Zuikaku*** (6th Attack Unit, led by Lt.Cmdr Shigekazu Shimazaki) reach Hickam and begin to shower the hangars, barracks and runway with 250kg bombs. Hangars 13 and 15 take direct hits, and are decimated.

---

Total enlisted men at Hickam, at 30 November 1941: 4,894 men, 486 officers.

Base Commander: Col. William E. Farthing.

**18TH BOMBARDMENT WING**
**5th Heavy Bombardment Group:**
4th Reconnaissance Squadron
B-17D (12)  [6 under repair]
23rd Bombardment Squadron
B-18A (6)  [2 under repair]
31st Bombardment Squadron
B-18A (5)  [2 under repair]
72nd Bombardment Squadron
B-18A (5)  [2 under repair]

**11th Heavy Bombardment Group:**
26th Bombardment Squadron
B-18A (6)  [2 under repair]
42nd Bombardment Squadron
B-18A (6)  [2 under repair]
98th Bombardment Squadron
B-18A (5)  [2 under repair]
58th Light Bombardment Squadron
A-20A (12)  [7 under repair]
**19th Transport Squadron:**
B-12A (3)  [2 under repair]; A-12 (2)

**DAMAGE TO HICKAM FIELD**
Of the 59 bombers at Hickam on the morning of 7 December 1941, 4 x B-17s, 12 x B-18s and 2 x A-20s were destroyed: 21 planes were put out of commission, and 19 survived intact.

The total Army Air Force losses in Oahu from both Japanese attacks were 163 killed, 336 wounded, 43 missing. Of these, total Army Air Force losses at Hickam Field were 121 killed, 274 wounded, 37 missing.

**KEY TO HANGARS**
A  Hangars 15 and 17
B  Hangars 11 and 13
C  Hangars 7 and 9
D  Hangars 3 and 5
E  Hangars 2 and 4

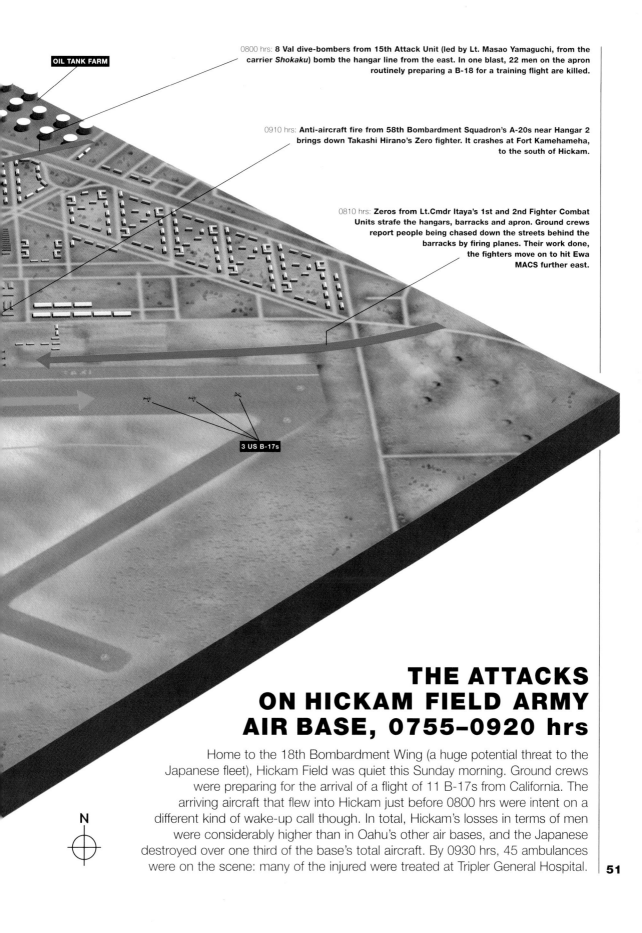

**OIL TANK FARM**

0800 hrs: **8 Val dive-bombers from 15th Attack Unit (led by Lt. Masao Yamaguchi, from the carrier *Shokaku*) bomb the hangar line from the east. In one blast, 22 men on the apron routinely preparing a B-18 for a training flight are killed.**

0910 hrs: **Anti-aircraft fire from 58th Bombardment Squadron's A-20s near Hangar 2 brings down Takashi Hirano's Zero fighter. It crashes at Fort Kamehameha, to the south of Hickam.**

0810 hrs: **Zeros from Lt.Cmdr Itaya's 1st and 2nd Fighter Combat Units strafe the hangars, barracks and apron. Ground crews report people being chased down the streets behind the barracks by firing planes. Their work done, the fighters move on to hit Ewa MACS further east.**

**3 US B-17s**

# THE ATTACKS ON HICKAM FIELD ARMY AIR BASE, 0755–0920 hrs

Home to the 18th Bombardment Wing (a huge potential threat to the Japanese fleet), Hickam Field was quiet this Sunday morning. Ground crews were preparing for the arrival of a flight of 11 B-17s from California. The arriving aircraft that flew into Hickam just before 0800 hrs were intent on a different kind of wake-up call though. In total, Hickam's losses in terms of men were considerably higher than in Oahu's other air bases, and the Japanese destroyed over one third of the base's total aircraft. By 0930 hrs, 45 ambulances were on the scene: many of the injured were treated at Tripler General Hospital.

N

The US Army Air Corps had all manner of aircraft at its various airfields, including this obsolete open cockpit P-26 Peashooter at Wheeler Field. Its lineage from the racing aircraft of the early 1930s is evident.

long flight from the mainland, they flew blindly into a turkey shoot. Some Japanese aircraft ignored the grounded planes and, guns blazing, made straight for the incoming B-17s. The latter broke formation and headed off in all directions to escape their attackers. Three Japanese Zeros latched on to Landon's tail as he landed, shot and shell bursting around him. Other B-17 pilots were under attack, from friend and foe alike, as they tried to land all over the island. All made it to one airfield or another. When the smoke cleared, more than half the aircraft at Hickam were burning or shattered hulks.

Station KGMB interrupted its broadcast and transmitted: 'All army, navy and marine personnel, report to duty!'

Back in the harbor, *West Virginia* was struck twice, the blows coming so close together that one felt almost like the aftershock of the other. She began to list strongly to port, when a third blast rocked her, setting her No. 3 turret aflame. Cpt. Bennion was nearly eviscerated by shrapnel and collapsed, mortally wounded. Lt.Cmdr Johnson and Mess Attendant Dorian Miller (fleet boxing champion) tended his wounds. He ordered them to leave, but Miller hefted him up and they got him to a pharmacist's mate who made him comfortable and answered questions about the battle until Bennion died moments later. Miller then manned a machine-gun in as cool a fashion as he boxed. Another explosion

rocked *West Virginia* seconds later. Before the end of the day she was to take six torpedoes and two bomb hits.

At 0812 hrs Kimmel sent a message to the Pacific Fleet and Washington DC: 'Hostilities with Japan commenced with air raid on Pearl Harbor.' Three minutes later KGMB transmitted another message, repeating the call for all military personnel to report to duty stations.

In the harbor, all had been caught unawares, like sitting ducks. However, through the smoke and flame came a sight to give hope to all the sailors and personnel witnessing the devastation: a destroyer had fought its way clear of the smoke and was heading towards the mouth of the harbor. The USS *Helm* was making her run to the open sea.

The *Arizona*'s bridge was aflame and she was settling like a rock. Her explosion showered the harbor with debris, body parts and survivors. Many men were hopelessly trapped below deck in an instant. Over 1,000 died with her in that devastating moment, including Adm. Kidd and Cpt. Van Valkenburg. Lt.Cmdr Fuqua realized that *Arizona* was 'no longer in fighting condition' and ordered survivors to abandon ship. *Arizona* endured at least eight bombs and torpedoes; as of 1032 hrs, the ship was a hulk. When she settled on the bottom, *Arizona* had lost over 1,200 men.

At 0817 hrs *Helm* exited Pearl Harbor and spotted a small sub outside the entrance. *Helm* fired on the sub but missed. The sub hit a reef, struggled, and freed itself, submerging while *Helm* fired fruitlessly.

The time was 0825 hrs. In Honolulu the fire department had been deluged with calls for assistance and had responded to Hickam Field. Enemy aircraft strafed the fire-fighting vehicles, killing three fire-fighters and wounding six. Five minutes later KGMB sent out a third call for military personnel to report to base. By 0845 hrs *Neosho* had cleared Battleship Row and the oil tanks on Ford Island. She reached Merry's Point in South-East Loch at 0852 hrs.

In Honolulu rumors abounded. Civilians, military personnel, government leaders, Hawaiian, Caucasian and Japanese-American, young and old, stood wide-eyed at the scene in the harbor. Some thought the explosions and low-flying aircraft were an Army Air Corps training exercise; others thought oil tanks on the base must have exploded. Still others realized that the island was under attack and feared imminent invasion. Many citizens watched the 'air show' over Pearl Harbor and Schofield, not realizing the situation. Stray rounds and a few bombs hit the city, jarring civilians out of their stupor. Police warned citizens to stay calm and return to their homes.

After getting underway from the West Loch, *Monaghan* and the seaplane tender *Curtiss* headed south towards the harbor entrance. Local radio stations sent out the first reports saying that Pearl Harbor was under attack by enemy aircraft with Rising Sun markings.

Adm. Kimmel was watching the battle when a spent bullet shattered his office window, hitting him in the chest and knocking him backwards a few steps. Men standing nearby were astounded to see Kimmel slowly bend over and pick up the spent round. He studied it for a while and then pronounced: 'It would have been merciful had it killed me.'

**LEFT When the SBDs from *Enterprise* arrived, some were shot down by friendly fire and others were attacked by Japanese aircraft. Many scattered, pursued by Zeros. Staff Sergeant Lee Embree aboard a B-17 photographed the scene. Some made it safely away, but this one evidently did not.**

Despite the element of total surprise, two US pilots, Lt. George Welch and Lt. Kenneth Taylor, managed to get airborne from Haleiwa Field in their P-40s – some of the very few who managed to do so. Dogfights broke out over the skies of Oahu. Welch and Taylor were among the few who took the fight to the Japanese, and who managed to contest control of the airspace. Meanwhile the Japanese attack continued relentlessly, as here at Hickam Field: the parked B-17s, B-18s and A-20s received a heavy pounding, as did the row of hangars.

# THE SECOND WAVE

There was no real break between the first and the second waves of attack, just a momentary pause in the battering before the rain of death resumed. Oily smoke streamed skywards from many of the ships; vessels listed or displayed rust-streaked bottoms when they capsized; and the incoming second wave could have used the smudge on the sky as a beacon, had it been unsure of the target area.

At Wheeler Field to the north of Pearl Harbor, P-40 Bs and Cs were lined up with the obsolete P-36s outside the hangars, as ordered by Gen. Short to protect them from sabotage. The element of complete surprise was the same, as the Japanese aircraft swept in to systematically attack ground targets; aircraft, hangars, base buildings, the EM club and the golf course. The attacks followed the same dreadful pattern: first bombers released payloads, then they climbed and joined the circling Zeros, then both dived, strafing the field and buildings. Men of the 14th Pursuit Wing sought to push undamaged aircraft to safety while Japanese aircraft dived on them repeatedly. Many wheels were shot flat, and hangars storing munitions were set ablaze.

**The battleships *West Virginia* and *Tennessee* were moored next to each other. Repeated Japanese aircraft struck both of them, wreathing the battleships and the vessels which aided them in billowing clouds of oily smoke.**

The *Nevada*, pictured after the attack. She suffered repeated hits, but Thomas, her acting commander, was a fighter: he tried to take her to sea. Japanese dive-bombers sought to sink her and block the channel, but the resourceful Thomas beached her to thwart them.

At 0810 hrs Cpt. Frank W. Ebey of the 55th Coast Artillery dropped the book he was reading when the first attack started and yelled for his sergeant to get the machine-guns working. By 0814 hrs the guns were set up on the tennis court and blazing away at the attackers. They hit one of the Zeros and it faltered and went down.

If the first wave was smooth and took little damage, the second wave bore the brunt of the US resistance. Although initially surprised and mauled, the remaining US air defenses were determined to even the score.

Two American pilots, lieutenants George Welch and Kenneth Taylor, had danced and then played poker the remainder of the evening before. Tired, they heard the first crackle of gunfire and thumps of distant bombs at 0800 hrs. Running outside, they saw low-flying aircraft with red Rising Suns on their wings. Calling Haleiwa Field in the north of Oahu, they ordered their P-40s readied, then they hopped into Taylor's car and sped towards the field. Japanese aircraft buzzed them as they drove, bullets chewing up the roadway. They raced down the winding road, not only to reach their aircraft, but to avoid strafing attacks. Perhaps if they could get aloft …

Taylor and Welch hopped into their readied aircraft and took off, some of the few defenders who were able to do so. Some historians have noted that Haleiwa Field was not attacked. Perhaps Taylor and Welch getting aloft dissuaded would-be attackers, or perhaps their later run-in diverted the planned air strike.

In the harbor USS *Alwyn* started seaward at 0828 hrs. Bombs splashed around her and she slowly surged forward, ordered to depart and rendezvous with *Enterprise.* A bomb fell just short of her fantail, slamming her stern into an anchor buoy and damaging one of her screws. Aboard, only ensigns commanded *Alwyn,* all other officers being ashore. She made the open sea at 0932 hrs. Her commander pursued and tried to catch up, following her out of harbor in a launch, but she did not stop for him for fear of Japanese submarines.

Col. Weddington at Bellows was ready for the attack. Earlier a lone strafer had sailed across the field and departed. Since then, men had rushed feverishly about dispersing the 86th Observation Squadron's O-47s and O-49s, and 44th Pursuit Squadron's P-40s an P-36s.

Schofield Barracks was under intense air attack. At 0825 hrs Lt. Stephen Saltzman, communications officer of the 98th Coastal Artillery, heard the scream of diving planes. He grabbed a Browning automatic rifle (BAR) and a couple of magazines and rushed outside. Sgt Lowell Klatt did likewise and followed him. A Zero was coming right at them, and they stood their ground, opening up with the BARs while the Zero's 7.7mm guns chewed up the ground. The pilot pulled up, avoiding high tension wires, and both men emptied their magazines at the Zero. It wobbled over the building, then lost altitude and crashed.

At 0850 hrs Lt.Cmdr Shimazaki's second wave arrived on the scene and deployed to attack pre-designated targets, while Fuchida was still flying over the smoking vessels and assessing damage. Fuchida briefly considered personally directing the attack, but he decided that Shimazaki was doing an excellent job. Besides, his assessment was needed by Nagumo, who would use it to decide about the third wave.

A mere four minutes later the second wave hit the stricken fleet and military bases with 54 high level bombers and 78 dive-bombers and 36 fighters. The fighters, whose mission was to secure air space control, met no airborne resistance and joined the fray by strafing US positions. Shimazaki's planes peeled off for their respective targets – Hickam, Ford Island and Kaneohe. Shindo took his fighters in. Half of them made for Hickam Field and Ford Island, while the other half headed west towards Kaneohe and then separated into two groups. One hit Bellows; the other first strafed the floatplane berth and then turned towards Wheeler to strafe it. Ground anti-aircraft fire was intense.

At the same time the battered battleship *Nevada* moved sluggishly away from her berth north-east of Ford Island. Smoke partly obscured visibility and her tortured boilers clawed their way towards the sea. The wind blew through her shattered bow, which sported a large gouge. Still,

## ATTACKS ON EWA MACS AND BELLOWS FIELD AIR BASES

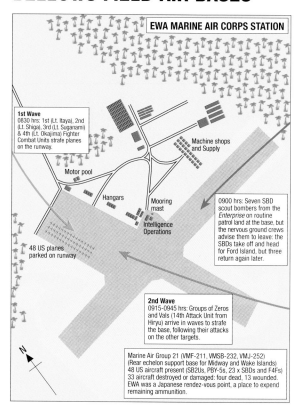

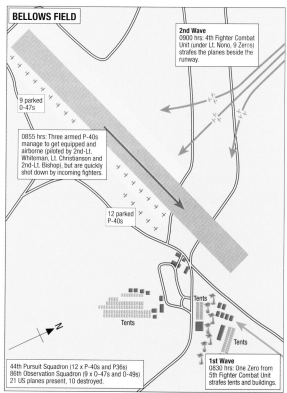

Bellows Field suffered some damage during the attack, as shown by the blown-off wing tip of this P-40. In the background a soldier wearing fatigues confers with airmen.

Thomas and Ruff were going to take her to sea, past the shattered and burning vessels on Battleship Row if they could.

Further north, in Pearl Harbor's East Loch, Lt.Cmdr Bill Burford of the destroyer *Monaghan* was moving her south-south-west, heading for the sea to find and support *Ward*. Enemy aircraft strafed her, smoke from damaged ships clouded the waterway, and other vessels determined to reach the safety of open sea were in various stages of getting underway and clogged the narrow seaward corridor. Ahead *Curtiss* was moving towards the mouth of the harbor and signaled *Monaghan* that a Japanese submarine had been sighted.

*Curtiss* fired on the sub at 0839 hrs. Noting *Curtiss'* actions, the *Monaghan* tried but could not bring her guns to bear: a moment later one of the watch reported seeing the twin-torpedo tubes of some craft breaking the surface. Other nearby craft fired at it and *Monaghan* set herself on a collision course with the sub. The sub was wounded and surfaced just in time for *Monaghan* to slice across it. *Monaghan* slammed along the side of the sub, which was pulled under her. After hitting the sub, *Monaghan* dropped depth charges on the spot. The submarine surfaced and shortly afterwards took hits from *Curtiss'* 5-in. and .50-cal. guns. One tore through the conning tower, no doubt killing the commander.

Acting quickly and despite the chance that he might damage his own stern, Burford put two depth charges overboard. Their explosions lifted *Monaghan*'s stern out of the water, but they blew the bow off the sub. In the confusion, *Monaghan* slammed into a dredge, sustaining light damage, but then the destroyer broke into the open sea. It was 0908 hrs.

At 0847 hrs *Blue* started for the mouth of the harbor. Two Japanese planes buzzed her and were met with .50-cal. fire. One wavered, smoked and crashed near the Pan American Airways Landing at Pearl City. Three-quarters of an hour later she

Japanese midget (two-man) subs were ferried to Pearl aboard larger Japanese subs. This one was dimpled by depth charges, rammed by *Monaghan* and consequently beached.

Kaneohe was attacked by Japanese aircraft which strafed not only the airstrip and hangars, but also PBYs moored dockside. Here a PBY patrol plane burns outside a hangar.

broke through to the open sea and began patrolling. There was a sound on sonar, and *Blue* responded with depth charges. A pattern of bubbles and an oily patina colored the waters for 200 feet, indicating a hit.

At 0900 hrs the 4th Fighter Unit struck Bellows Field. Lt. Nono's nine aircraft hit in three waves of three, each wave formed as an arrowhead, blasting aircraft on the ground and those struggling to get aloft. O-47s were shredded by machine-gun fire, a fuel truck was ablaze, and one fighter of the 44th Squadron was downed while lifting off. One B-17 was coming in. It touched down midway on the landing strip, and then ran out of runway, resulting in three wounded crewmen. All nine Zeros strafed the battered plane past the end of the runway, but the bomber

This China Clipper was moored in much the same manner as Kaneohe's PBYs, less than 25 yards offshore. Unlike the PBYs which were shot to pieces in the water or on runways, the Clipper was unharmed in the attack.

was already out of action and they were wasting ammunition on what was a hulk. Two pilots of the 44th were soon airborne, but having just taken off, they were easy prey for the Japanese fighters, which came in on their tails and shot them down before they could gain altitude. One 44th pilot survived when his airplane splashed down near the beach and he waded ashore from its wreckage.

With Bellows in disarray, Iida's and Nono's planes began their attack on Kaneohe at 0900 hrs, which was also being pounded by heavy horizontal bombing. When they arrived, bombs were falling around the hangars. Aircraft in the hangars exploded and burned in place.

Gordon Jones and his brother Earl had been stationed at Kaneohe on December 2 1941, and yet only five days later they were to have their baptism of fire. Between the first and second wave, they were kept busy trying to extinguish fires and moving less damaged planes to safer locations. When it began, they had no reason to suspect that the second wave would be any different to the first, as Gordon recalls: 'When this new wave of fighters attacked, we were ordered to run and take shelter. Most of us ran to our nearest steel hangar … this bomb attack made us aware that the hangar was not a safe place to be … several of us ran north to an abandoned Officer's Club and hid under it until it too was machine-gunned. I managed to crawl out and took off my white uniform, because I was told that men in whites were targets. I then climbed under a large thorny bush … for some reason I felt much safer at this point than I had during the entire attack.' For most of the men at Kaneohe, there was little else they could do but take cover until the devastating assault had passed.

Chief Ordnanceman John William Finn, a Navy veteran of 15 years service, was in charge of looking after the squadron's machine-guns at Kaneohe, but Sunday 7 December was his rest day. The sound of machine-gun fire awoke him rudely though, and he rapidly drove from his quarters to the hangars and his ordnance shop to see what was happening. Maddened by the scene of chaos and devastion that he saw, he set up and manned both a .30-cal. and a .50-cal. machine-gun in a completely exposed section of the parking ramp, despite the attention of heavy enemy strafing fire. He later recalled: 'I was so mad I wasn't scared'. Finn was hit several times as he valiantly returned the Japanese fire, but he continued to man the gun, as other sailors supplied him with ammunition. John Finn was later awarded the Congressional Medal of Honor for his valor and courage beyond the call of duty in this action. Even after receiving inadequate first aid treatment, he insisted on returning to his post to supervise the re-arming of the returning PBYs that had escaped the devastation at Kaneohe.

Firemen trying to fight the blazes also came under strafing attack. One fire truck was hit and crashed into a hangar, exploding and setting fire to the hangar. The mission was not to be a complete success for Lt. Iida though: his plane (BI-151) suddenly waffled, having been hit by US fire, and his engine changed pitch. Iida knew he was in trouble. He banked, signaling to a fellow pilot and pointing down to the ground, indicating that he was going to crash into the enemy in what would in later months be termed a *kamikaze* attack. Iida's Zero skimmed over the armory building (probably the intended aim of his dive) to crash into the hill behind, near the officer's quarters. Flipping, it skidded upside down before jamming into the embankment. Some believed Iida was probably dead before his plane hit the ground. Arthur W. Price, stationed at Kaneohe that morning, recalls the plane crashing: 'We managed to recover some paperwork from his plane. Included was a map ... We later learned that it indicated our water tank was a fuel farm. Those pilots had just peppered the hell out of that tank during the attack but couldn't set it on fire. I think that sort of confused them'.

19 US servicemen were killed in the attack on Kaneohe that day: they were buried the following day on Mokopu Point on the east side of the NAS. The bodies were later all sent back to the US. A ceremony was also held for Lt. Fusata Iida on 8 December at Kaneohe. His body was sent back to Japan after the war.

Despite the loss of Iida's and two other planes, the attack on Kaneohe achieved its aims. Three PBYs were out on patrol, but of those remaining, 33 were destroyed. Iida's fellow fighters re-formed, and flew towards Wheeler.

En route holes opened in their aircraft – they were under attack! US fighters with blazing machine-guns were coming after them. Lieutenants Welch and Taylor – and others from 47th Pursuit Squadron at Haleiwa – were there, weaving and diving, taking the battle to the enemy in P-36s and P-40s. A group of pilots from 46th Pursuit Squadron, including 1st-Lt. Lewis Sanders, had also managed to get airborne in their P-36s from Wheeler, as the Zeros arrived to attack the base: they took off virtually into the path of the approaching Japanese fighters. Dogfights erupted all around. Welch and Taylor made their presence known. Taylor dropped into a group of seven or eight Japanese aircraft, first firing at the one ahead, and taking fire from one behind him. Welch later recalled how he 'shot down one right on Lt. Taylor's tail.'

Wheeler Field was a primary target in the Japanese attack plan. Once the ships were in flames, Americans would think of retaliation. If airfields were decimated, there would be little or no retaliation. Flood had ordered nearly 100 U-shaped bunkers built to house aircraft and protect them from air attack. Short, however, had ordered that planes be massed to protect them from sabotage. There were no trenches and no anti-aircraft, as that was not Flood's responsibility but the Department's. Wheeler Field was a sitting duck. When Japanese aircraft reached it, American aircraft were neatly grouped on runways and aprons. The Japanese aircraft banked and came in low, guns blazing, dropping bombs on sitting targets. Planes, quarters, PX, the administration building and the golf course were shredded by gunfire and bombs. As Flood said, the attackers were so close 'I could even see the gold in their teeth.'

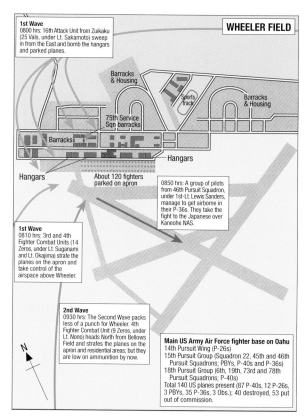

ABOVE **Details of the attack waves that struck Wheeler Field air base.**

Okajima's fighters had arrived at Wheeler in the first wave to find others already there, the air a canopy of Japanese attackers. He decided to find fresh targets, so he headed towards Ewa Field to hit the marines. They made repeated passes at the American aircraft on the ground. As at Wheeler, bullets ruptured fuel tanks, which ignited. Fuel spilled from bullet holes, and rivulets of aviation gasoline streamed from damaged aircraft to others which were crackling and threatening to explode. The fire truck tried to reach the aircraft to salvage ammunition and guns, but Japanese strafers blew out its tires and it ground to a halt.

Fuel spilled in streams, setting fire to tents and even to the sand which soaked it up. The second wave of attack came just over half an hour later, savaging tents, and burning hulks, the hospital, other buildings and personnel. One marine fired his .45 at Japanese aircraft in frustration.

On the ground a group of marines manhandled a scout plane, used it as a machine-gun platform, and opened fire on their attackers, shooting down one Japanese aircraft. The Japanese strike force roared away, leaving Wildcats blazing, scout bombers burning and utility aircraft destroyed. Their losses? One dive-bomber and three Zeros.

Shindo and Nikaido (1st and 2nd Fighter Units) headed to their assigned targets: Hickam Field and Ford Island. Once there, they would blast a path for the horizontal bombers. Anti-aircraft fire forced Shindo to fight for altitude to protect his aircraft. The bombers arrived, laying a carpet of explosives on Hickam. When anti-aircraft was occupied with the high altitude aircraft, Shindo brought his fighters down to just above

BELOW **The attack on Kaneohe NAS was particularly devastating, and the base suffered a proportionately high level of damage. A combination of strafing attacks by Zeros and high-level bombing from Kates ensured that almost all the PBYs stationed there were destroyed. (By kind permission of Mr John S. Kennedy, author of The Forgotten Warriors of Kaneohe.)**

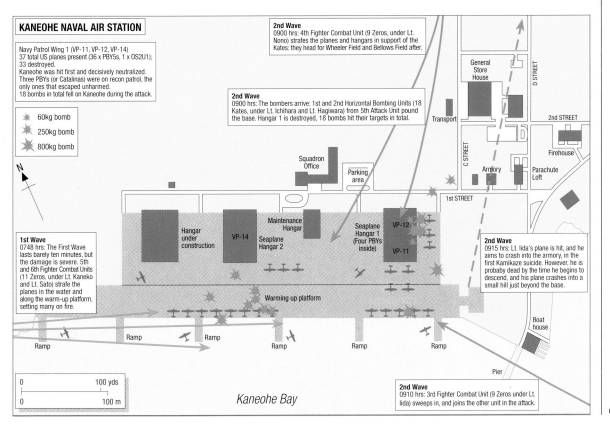

### KANEOHE NAVAL AIR STATION

Navy Patrol Wing 1 (VP-11, VP-12, VP-14)
37 total US planes present (36 x PBY5s, 1 x OS2U1);
33 destroyed.
Kaneohe was hit first and decisively neutralized.
Three PBYs (or Catalinas) were on recon patrol, the only ones that escaped unharmed.
18 bombs in total fell on Kaneohe during the attack.

* 60kg bomb
* 250kg bomb
* 800kg bomb

**2nd Wave**
0900 hrs: 4th Fighter Combat Unit (9 Zeros, under Lt. Nono) strafes the planes and hangars in support of the Kates: they head for Wheeler Field and Bellows Field after.

**2nd Wave**
0900 hrs: The bombers arrive: 1st and 2nd Horizontal Bombing Units (18 Kates, under Lt. Ichihara and Lt. Hagiwara) from 5th Attack Unit pound the base. Hangar 1 is destroyed, 18 bombs hit their targets in total.

General Store House

D STREET

Transport

2nd STREET

C STREET

Squadron Office

Parking area

Firehouse

Armory

Parachute Loft

1st STREET

**1st Wave**
0748 hrs: The First Wave lasts barely ten minutes, but the damage is severe. 5th and 6th Fighter Combat Units (11 Zeros, under Lt. Kaneko and Lt. Sato) strafe the planes in the water and along the warm-up platform, setting many on fire.

Hangar under construction

VP-14

Maintenance Hangar

Seaplane Hangar 2

Seaplane Hangar 1 (Four PBYs inside)

VP-12

VP-11

**2nd Wave**
0915 hrs: Lt. Iida's plane is hit, and he aims to crash into the armory, in the first Kamikaze suicide. However, he is probaby dead by the time he begins to descend, and his plane crashes into a small hill just beyond the base.

Warming up platform

Ramp

Ramp

Ramp

Ramp

Ramp

Ramp

Boat house

Pier

N

Kaneohe Bay

**2nd Wave**
0910 hrs: 3rd Fighter Combat Unit (9 Zeros under Lt. Iida) sweeps in, and joins the other unit in the attack.

0 | 100 yds
0 | 100 m

Mobile anti-aircraft guns were deployed at Kaneohe during the week but taken back to army bases on the weekend. Kaneohe was virtually defenseless when Japanese aircraft began their strafing runs.

rooftop level, making a pass on the installation and strafing dispersed aircraft, technical buildings and offices.

The bombers were rocked by anti-aircraft fire. They sought and hit the mess hall again, as well as hangars 13 and 15. Above the clouds, they flew through the barrage of anti-aircraft to drop their deadly cargo.

At their altitude, proper visual target identification was exacting under the best conditions, and now they were flying over a smudgepot while shells burst around them and tracers licked at their wing tips. More than one bomber returned to its carrier with wind whistling through multiple bullet holes, but they all made it back.

Egusa's dive bombers, carrying their 250kg bombs, had the worst of it. Their job was dirty: finish off any unfinished business and get any battleships the first wave had missed. They had no element of surprise with them: the Americans were ready, armed and angry. As soon as they reached Oahu, flak began reaching up with greedy fingers, closing its grasp and threatening to unnerve many Japanese dive-bomber pilots. Lt. Abe commented: 'AA barrages began … to close in. This gave me the shivers.'

Visibility was abysmal. The careful plans were abandoned, and instead Egusa's flyers decided to pick any target they had the opportunity to fire upon. Through the smoke and flames they dived, coming down low to try and pick out targets. They were not fearful while attacking, but more than one admitted to feeling shaky once they had dropped their bomb and headed towards their rendezvous.

Pearl Harbor was filled with burning oil, its smudgy plumes darkening the skies above the twisted metal hulks of American warships. Stragglers and survivors were taken to aid centers or headquarters. In momentary lulls between bomb blasts, when there was no anti-aircraft and just the soft whoosh and crackle of flames, it was as if a sudden deafness had affected everyone.

Through the oily smoke poked a battered bow: *Nevada* was making her run south. Minutes earlier she had picked up a few floating survivors of *Arizona* when she was gaining momentum. Only a few vessels moved in the harbor, but she was one. She may have been down, but she was not out.

Egusa's Vals saw *Nevada* at 0850 hrs and realized what she was attempting. This was too good to be true: a target, a battleship at that, and one which could bottle up the harbor if they could sink her. Coming lower, they flew directly over *Neosho*, homing on *Nevada*. She had taken several hits but was still moving when another attack at 0905 hrs singled her out for destruction. Bombs fell near her, their explosions sending geysers of water sluicing over her decks. It appeared that she would escape without further damage when one bomb exploded in front of her forecastle, slaying many sailors and jarring the whole vessel with a shudder which slammed teeth shut and knocked some men off their feet.

Thomas knew his peril. *Nevada* responded with difficulty, and he realized she was taking on water. If she went down here, she would partially block the harbor and make undamaged vessels still in the harbor sitting targets, little more than fish in a barrel. He gave orders to turn to port and sluggishly she reacted. At 0910 hrs her bow plowed into shore at Hospital Point, knocking sailors sprawling, grounding *Nevada*. Her bow looked as if it had been gnawed off, and her superstructure was partly buckled – but she had not sunk! It was a minor victory, but every vessel denied the enemy was one more vessel which could later take the fight to them.

Meanwhile at 0902 hrs other dive-bombers dropped low and made passes at *Pennsylvania*'s dry dock. One bomb missed *Pennsylvania* but hit *Shaw* and blew off her entire bow. Another dive-bomber put a hit on *Pennsylvania*'s starboard side at 0907 hrs, doing a relatively small amount of structural damage but killing 18 and wounding 30 officers and men. Nearby *Cassin* and *Downes* were bombed. Soon they were aflame and had to be abandoned. Just minutes later *Cassin* was wrenched with a magazine explosion that rolled her port side against *Downes*. In the

**Wheeler Field and nearby Schofield Barracks were raked repeatedly by Japanese aircraft but remained surprisingly usable. The smoke comes from burning aircraft on the landing strip.**

Chief Ordnanceman John William Finn was in charge of the squadron's machine-guns at Kaneohe NAS. Despite great danger to himself, he set up both a .30-cal. and a .50-cal. machine-gun in an exposed section of the parking ramp, as others (including 2nd Cl. PO Robert Peterson, shown here in this scene drawn from contemporary accounts) supplied him with ammunition. Finn moved between the two, but stayed longer on the .50-cal. due to the ease of re-loading and the weight of its firepower. Despite being wounded several times, he inflicted a heavy toll on the attackers, as bullets ripped through wings and fusilages. Lt. Iida's Zero, tail no. B1-151, was one of those hit, and crashed behind the armory.

harbor at 0930 hrs, the USS *Shaw* bucked like a bronco when multiple explosions shook her, sending a tower of debris skyward that fell everywhere.

Chaos ruled the basin. Burning oil floated towards *California*; *Maryland* struggled to free herself inboard of *Oklahoma*, which had capsized; *Arizona* smoldered; *Nevada* had broken free, but at a terrible price.

Dive-bombers singled out larger ships. *Raleigh* survived the first wave but was wracked with two explosions aft at 0908 hrs. One bomb passed through the deck and missed *Raleigh*'s aviation fuel tanks by less than four yards. *Raleigh* reeled and threatened to capsize. Only by hard work did her commander keep her upright and afloat.

*Argonne*, *Vestal* and *Oglala* were in trouble. Fire threatened *Vestal* and she had to move or risk immolation. A tug nosed the repair ship away from the burning *Arizona*. *Vestal* moved heavily through the water and began to list starboard. At 0905 hrs Young said *Vestal* was 'in bad shape – we had better beach her'. At 0945 hrs she nosed onto a coral reef at Aiea.

© *Jim Laurier* A.S.A.A.
3·99

This scary sight was seen by those at Pearl Harbor, as a Japanese Val with open dive brakes banked and came towards them. Black anti-aircraft dots the sky, but the Val flies through it unharmed. Note the proximity to the camera: many Vals came in very low and fast, a factor depending on the bravery and skill of the pilot.

*Oglala* was not so fortunate. Moored outboard of *Helena* at TenTen Pier, she had taken what they had thrown at her and was slowly listing. At 0930 hrs her decks were too angled to walk on and Furlong ordered the crew to abandon ship. Soon after she capsized, settling on her port side.

The cruiser *Honolulu* came under attack at 0920 hrs. Egusa's dive-bombers pounded the berth (B17) with several bombs; one near miss caused considerable flooding aboard. Concussion from the underwater blast was so strong that *St Louis*, which was berthed east of her (at B21), bounced from the shock wave.

At about 0932 hrs Lt.Cmdr Pullen, CO of the destroyer *Reid*, rushed through the savaged base towards the harbor, his heart heavy as he saw the ships burning and foundering. How badly mauled was *Reid*? He took his launch out to the ship and was surprised to have the officer of the deck tell him that everything was under control; then the chief engineer said that *Reid* would be able to get underway in about 30 minutes.

*St Louis'* commander, Cpt. Rood, had her make way, and she began to back out. At 0940 hrs, with her engines full astern, she neared the channel. A cable securing the dredge at the south end of Ford Island blocked *St Louis'* way. Rood ordered full speed ahead and plowed through the cable which parted. Down the channel she sped, disregarding the normal eight-knot speed limit in harbor and certain that at any moment Japanese aircraft could sight her and attack. *St Louis'* speed crept up to 22 knots and she cleared the harbor at 1004 hrs. Rood allowed himself the luxury of a deep breath when they reached the sea.

No doubt Rood thought *St Louis* was clear, but then the watch saw two torpedo wakes closing with her stern. He ordered her on an immediate evasion course, and an explosion rattled her when the torpedoes hit a coral reef. The midget sub surfaced and *St Louis'* gun crews opened fire, their shots penetrating the sub's conning tower, destroying her. *St Louis* was the last ship to leave Pearl Harbor during the attack.

Seen from Ford Island, a damaged *Nevada* is down at the bow but her funnel is smoking as she moves away from Ford and down the channel, attempting to reach the relative safety of the open sea.

While *Nevada* (her turrets visible to the bottom right) battled shipboard fires, a tug came alongside to give aid (foreground to the right). A direct magazine hit on the destroyer *Shaw* sent flames and debris skyrocketing.

After bombing the harbor Egusa's men flew towards Ford, Hickam and Ewa to strafe the airfields and buildings. Earlier in the day observers at Ewa had sighted Japanese aircraft before the attack on the naval basin. At Ewa Ofuchi's men flew low, guns blazing, and then they came under aerial attack from Welch and Taylor. Several Japanese planes went down, and Ofuchi broke off the combat. At the conclusion of this second dogfight, the two Americans claimed seven Japanese aircraft between them.

When the Japanese attacked, Battleship Row became a shooting gallery. *Oklahoma* (left) has capsized, *Maryland* is behind her, and a burning *West Virginia* (right) has sunk next to a damaged *Tennessee.*

The American fighters at Hickam were sitting ducks. When one was hit, the volatile aviation fuel ignited, sending up a fountain of flame. Like as not, the adjacent aircraft was damaged and its fuel was also leaking. A second later it too would ignite, damaging the next aircraft, and so on down the line until the runway was lined with blazing aircraft. American aircraft on the runways were defenseless.

Shimazaki's Kates hit Hickam and were joined by dive-bombers who helped strafe hangars and aircraft on the runway. The B-17s absorbed a great deal of damage, but showed once more why there were called 'Flying Fortresses'. Having little more to do and needing to reach the rendezvous, Shimazaki's men headed away from the airfield.

After a single pass at Hickam, Shindo broke off in his Zero and flew recon, studying the damage and assessing the effectiveness of the Japanese attack. Flying at 300m, he eyed the devastation. When he returned to *Akagi*, his report to Genda would be succinct: 'Inflicted much damage.'

At 1100 hrs, Cmdr Fuchida began his recon and assessment flight over Oahu. Carefully he noted which ship positions were burning, which had capsized or were now low in the water, and which appeared unharmed. Fuchida stayed over the harbor, observing and rounding up stragglers, despite his damaged aircraft. When the last aircraft of the latest wave turned east, Fuchida looked at the sun overhead and headed towards *Akagi*.

All over the island, radio stations urged civilians to get off the roads, go home, clear the streets, get under cover, declaring that this attack was 'the Real McCoy'. A bomb fell near Governor Poindexter's house, sending up a shower of earth and rattling doors and windows.

Lt.Cmdr W. Specht saw all of his 12 PT boats were undamaged, both those at the sub base and those near *Ramapo*. His six functional torpedo boats got underway from the sub base and maneuvered around the debris in the harbor, patrolling, picking up wounded and drifting sailors and taking them to shore, where they were transferred to hospitals or returned to their ships.

At 1000 hrs aircraft of the first wave returned to the task force and began landing on *Akagi*, *Kaga* and other carriers positioned 190 miles north of Oahu. Back on the island Governor Poindexter issued a state of emergency for the entire Hawaiian territory, first to newspapers, and 15 minutes later via a radio broadcast. Reports of civilian casualties started coming in from hospitals, and by 1042 hrs all radio stations had shut off their transmitters to prevent them being used as homing beacons by attacking aircraft. Meanwhile Gen. Short conferred with Poindexter about placing the entire territory under martial law while the first false reports of invading enemy troops began circulating and all schools were ordered closed. That night, and every night in the near future, there would be a blackout in Hawaii.

Surviving American aircraft took off from damaged fields and began the search for their attackers at about midday. They flew north but did not sight the Japanese task force. At 1230 hrs the Honolulu police, aided by the FBI, descended on the Japanese embassy, where they found consular personnel near wastepaper baskets full of ashes and still-burning documents.

RIGHT **Details of the damage inflicted on the *Nevada*.**

BELOW **The path through the harbor of the *Nevada*'s attempted escape.**

One of the most significant moments during the the attack on Pearl Harbor was the gallant sortie of the *USS Nevada*. The sight of the ship moving Battleship Row roused the morale of those who watching, in the US navy's darkest hours. The s assault that she underwent during her break for resulted in the death of numerous crew members, Chief Boatswain Edwin J. Hill, who cast off *Nevad* before swimming back to the ship.

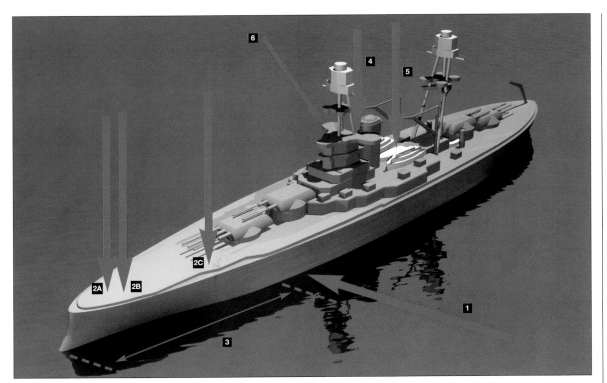

1 At 0803 hrs, two torpedo planes attack the *Nevada* while she is still berthed at the north-east end of Battleship Row. Gunners on board manage to shoot both of the planes down, but one manages to launch a torpedo and scores a direct hit on the port bow, at frame 40. The blast shakes the whole ship, and she begins to take on water. This constitutes the most significant damage done to the *Nevada* during the whole of the Pearl Harbor attack.

2 0900 hrs: Japanese bombers spot the *Nevada* as she passes TenTen Pier in her break for safety, and swoop down on her from the south-west and south-east in a split formation (the idea is to

confuse and split the American AA fire). Only the planes that attack 'in the sun' manage to score hits with their bombs. The planes, led by Lt. Saburo Makino, target her foreturret and midsection. During this intense period of attack, she sustains three direct hits from Japanese Val dive-bombers in her fore (**2A**, **2B** and **2C**). She continues to take on water, but presses ahead.

3 Fire engulfs all the compartments on the second and main decks in the fore of the ship following the direct hits scored in this area. It will continue to burn fiercely for 48 hours.

4 0907 hrs: Lt. Yamada's team of dive-bombers take over the attack and swoop in on the

stricken ship. A fourth bomb hits the forecastle, causing considerable damage and costing the lives of several crew members.

5 A fifth bomb hits the *Nevada* shortly after, at the base of her rear tripod mast.

6 A powder fire has broken out in her gun casemate, to starboard of her rear tripod mast. The *Nevada* is by now sitting low in the water. Her acting captain realizes she is in danger of blocking the channel by sinking where she is, so the decision is taken to beach her on the near-by Hospital Point. The time is just after 0910 hrs.

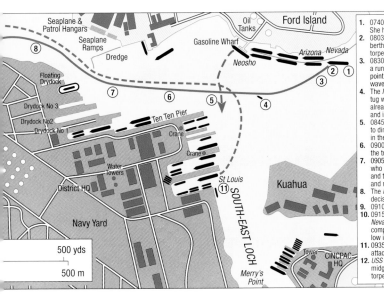

1. 0740 hrs: the *Nevada* was the last ship on Battleship Row, moored by herself. She had one boiler up and running, which enabled her to get moving.
2. 0803 hrs, two Japanese torpedo planes attack her port bow while she is still at berth. Gunners on board bring the planes down, but one manages to launch a torpedo that hits her port bow, at frame #40. She begins to take on water.
3. 0830 hrs, and Lt.Com. Francis J. Thomas (acting commander) decides to make a run for the sea - the damage done to the adjacent *Arizona* presses home the point. She edges herself out at 0840 hrs, in the brief lull between the attack waves.
4. The *Nevada* is trailed throughout her sortie attempt by the tug boat *YT-153*: the tug was ordered to help her out of her berth, but found that the *Nevada* had already got underway. The little tug follows her all the way down the channel, and is first on the scene when she eventually beaches.
5. 0845 hrs, the tanker *Neosho* pulls away from the fuel tanks at the gasoline wharf, to diminish the danger of a direct hit - the *Nevada* and her do well not to collide in the middle of the channel. The second wave bombs have begun to fall.
6. 0900 hrs, and *Nevada* passes TenTen Pier, having navigated the channel alone: the trickiest part of the exit route lies ahead though.
7. 0905 hrs, and the *Nevada* comes under intense attack from the Vals of Lt. Makino, who have spotted her run for safety. The planes come in from the south-west and the south-east, to split the anti-aircraft fire. She sustains five hits to her fore and mid section.
8. The *Nevada* is now taking on water, and blazing midships and forward: the decision is taken to beach her, or else risk blocking the channel.
9. 0910 hrs, the *Nevada* beaches on Hospital Point, bow-first.
10. 0915 hrs, and the strong outbound current in the harbor's channel catches the *Nevada*'s stern and pulls her out into the channel once more: she swings completely round. After the attack she is tugged to Buoy No.19, where she lies low in the water, still burning.
11. 0935 hrs, and the USS *St. Louis* has also got underway in the confusion of the attack, slipping away from her berth in the repair basin of the Navy Yard.
12. USS *St. Louis* moves towards the open sea: later she is targeted by a Japanese midget submarine at the mouth of the channel, but escapes being hit by the torpedo launched.

Cmdr Fuchida touched down at 1300 hrs aboard the *Akagi*. He discussed launching the third wave with Adm. Nagumo, but Nagumo believed they had done well enough and decided not to launch another attack. At 1330 hrs *Akagi* sent a message to other vessels in the task force, telling them to withdraw.

Fuchikami delivered the message from Washington to Gen. Short's headquarters at 1145 hrs. It still had to be decoded and would not be seen by Short for another three hours. Almost seven hours after the attack had started, and easily seven and a half hours too late to be of any use, word of the now-past danger reached Short.

ABOVE **Looking down the dry dock at TenTen Pier, *Cassin* and *Downes* (center rear) are smoldering. *Helena* sits beside the pier, and the dry docked *Pennsylvania* is visible in the background. In the center, the minelayer *Oglala* has capsized.**

Japanese losses were minimal – negligible – in view of the victory they had won: 185 killed, one captured. American losses were staggering: 2,403 casualties (2,008 Navy, 218 Army, 109 Marines and 68 civilians) and 1,178 were wounded (710 Navy, 364 Army, 69 Marines and 35 civilians).

The *Arizona* saw the greatest loss of life, accounting for half the naval casualties. Losses included men from 44 states, the District of Columbia, Guam, Hawaii, the Philippines and Canada. As a result of Pearl Harbor, 16 Congressional Medals of Honor, 51 Navy Crosses, 53 Silver Crosses, four Navy and Marine Corps Medals, one Distinguished Flying Cross, four Distinguished Service Crosses, 1 Distinguished Service Medal and 3 Bronze Stars were awarded for the 110 minutes of combat. A tally of vessels shows all eight battleships sunk or heavily damaged, testifying to the accuracy of Japanese attacks; three cruisers damaged; four destroyers damaged; one minelayer sunk; and two auxiliaries sunk or capsized and one heavily damaged. The US lost 169 aircraft (92 Navy and 77 Army) and 150 were damaged (31 Navy and 128 Army).

## Japanese damage assessments

Fuchida flew over the harbor and recorded visible damage; once back aboard *Akagi*, he compared his notes with others' observations. Those aboard *Akagi* reported that bombers had hit four battleships, and

The devastation was immense: this shows a close-up of *Downes'* burnt hulk in dry dock; *Cassin* is capsized next to her. The super-structure in the background belongs to the battleship *Pennsylvania*.

Just after 0900 hrs, the *Nevada* passed TenTen Pier in her run for safety
towards the open sea. She had already sustained one torpedo hit at
berth, but now the second wave of Japanese planes (Val dive-bombers,
led by Lt. Saburo Makino from the carrier *Kaga*) swooped in to attack her.
Some came from the south-west, some attacked her from the south-east,
the aim being to split the American AA fire. The attack was concentrated
and she was hit several times. Thomas, her acting commander, decide to
beach her on Hospital Point shortly afterwards, to avoid the risk of
blocking the channel and preventing other ships from escaping.

although the 3rd Group's success could not be verified because of cloud cover, they believed they had inflicted one hit on a capital ship. Eleven torpedoes had struck home on one of three battleships. Dive-bombers had not been able to assess damage to battleships accurately because of smoke and fire, although one *Omaha* class cruiser (CL) was a known hit. *Akagi*'s fighters had shot down a B-17, a trainer and a transport, and of 40 aircraft on Hickam Field, 23 were ablaze while the remaining seven were seriously damaged. At Ewa over 30 aircraft had been damaged or destroyed.

*Kaga*'s pilots reported four torpedo hits each on *Arizona* and *Tennessee*. Bombers damaged the fore of *Arizona*, put two hits on *California* and one on *Maryland*. Clouds had interfered with observation of all attacks, and dive-bombers hit two battleships and certainly dropped one on *California*. Two enemy aircraft had been shot down, one was damaged by strafing and many on their target airfields were on fire after the mission.

*Hiryu* and *Soryu* reported six torpedo hits on a battleship with a cage mast, three hits on another battleship, which sank at once, two hits on another battleship and one on a cruiser. Bombing had sunk one battleship instantaneously; two bombs had landed on another battleship, causing a mighty explosion, six on three other battleships, and five on a heavy cruiser. Dive-bombers put five hits on light cruisers and one on a docked destroyer. They had set 20 aircraft at Wheeler ablaze (including four light bombers and a flying boat) and destroyed four hangars; at Ewa they had set 60 grounded aircraft ablaze, and at Kaneohe, 10.

*Shokaku* and *Zuikaku*'s planes reported destroying two flying boat hangars and one for bombers at Ford Island. At Kaneohe they had hit nearly 50 flying boats and their hangar, and they had burned 80 per cent of the hangars at Wheeler Field and three aircraft at Bellows Field. At Hickam their attack had set seven hangars ablaze.

Confusion because of multiple and overlapping attack responsibilities had commanders duplicate results given by other commanders.

**USS *Raleigh* was damaged during the attack. Shortly afterwards pontoons were used to keep her upright so she could be repaired and refitted. *Utah*'s hull is capsized to the right of the tug.**

**The air attack left Wheeler Field in ruins. Here are the remains of aircraft hangars and shattered shells of airplanes including a P-40 and a twin-engine amphibian.**

Still, the message was clear. The attacks had been very successful.

## The real damage

Specific damage inflicted by the Japanese was staggering. Every battleship was badly damaged. Most major vessels had been shot up. Even detail reports of damage are conflicting because of the fog of war. One thing is certain: only the carriers which were absent were unscathed. Actual damage to the fleet and the subsequent fate of the ships was as follows:

**Although capable of assimilating vast amounts of damage, grounded B-17s fared no better than any other aircraft on the landing strip when faced with Japanese direct hits. This B-17 at Hickam's Hangar 5 shows the aftermath and destruction of the Japanese thrust.**

*Arizona* BB39, one torpedo and eight bomb hits, sunk; converted into memorial for those who died at Pearl Harbor.

*California* BB44, two torpedo hits, one bomb hit, sunk; later raised.

*Maryland* BB46, two bomb hits, damaged; repaired and modernized.

*Nevada* BB36, one torpedo hit, five bomb hits, heavily damaged; run aground, repaired and modernized.

*Oklahoma* BB37, five (possibly more) torpedo hits, capsized; raised and scrapped.

*Pennsylvania* BB38, one bomb hit, damaged; repaired.

*Tennessee* BB43, two bomb hits, damaged; repaired.

*West Virginia* BB48, two bomb hits, five to seven torpedo hits, sunk; raised, repaired and modernized.

*Helena* CL50, one torpedo hit, heavily damaged; repaired.

*Honolulu* CL48, one near bomb hit with collateral damage; repaired.

*Raleigh* CL7, one torpedo and one bomb hit, heavily damaged; repaired and refitted.

*Shaw* DD373, three bomb hits, bow blown off in explosion.

*Cassin* DD372, one bomb hit, one near miss, heavily damaged; rebuilt.

*Downes* DD375, two bomb hits, heavily damaged; rebuilt.

*Helm* DD388, one bomb near by, damaged; continued tour of duty, repaired on return.

*Oglala* CM4, one torpedo, sunk; raised and repaired.

*Curtiss* AV4, one bomb hit, damaged; repaired.

*Sotoyomo* YT9, sunk; raised and repaired.

*Utah* AG16, two torpedo hits, capsized; left at bottom of naval basin.

*Vestal* AR4, two bomb hits, heavily damaged; grounded, refloated and repaired.

*YFD-2* sunk; raised and repaired.

## US aircraft losses

Bellows Field 10;
Ewa MACS 33;
Ford Island 26;
Hickam Field 18;
Kaneohe 33;
Wheeler Field 40;
USS *Enterprise* 5;
Four B-17s destroyed.

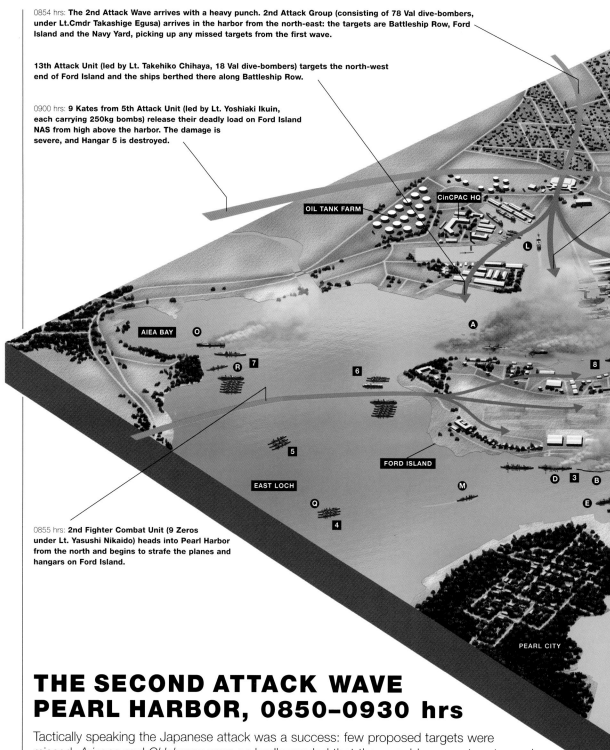

**0854 hrs:** The 2nd Attack Wave arrives with a heavy punch. 2nd Attack Group (consisting of 78 Val dive-bombers, under Lt.Cmdr Takashige Egusa) arrives in the harbor from the north-east: the targets are Battleship Row, Ford Island and the Navy Yard, picking up any missed targets from the first wave.

**13th Attack Unit (led by Lt. Takehiko Chihaya, 18 Val dive-bombers)** targets the north-west end of Ford Island and the ships berthed there along Battleship Row.

**0900 hrs:** 9 Kates from 5th Attack Unit (led by Lt. Yoshiaki Ikuin, each carrying 250kg bombs) release their deadly load on Ford Island NAS from high above the harbor. The damage is severe, and Hangar 5 is destroyed.

OIL TANK FARM

CinCPAC HQ

**L**

**A**

AIEA BAY

**O**

**R** **7**

**6**

**8**

**5**

FORD ISLAND

**D** **3** **B**

EAST LOCH

**M**

**Q**

**E**

**4**

**0855 hrs:** 2nd Fighter Combat Unit (9 Zeros under Lt. Yasushi Nikaido) heads into Pearl Harbor from the north and begins to strafe the planes and hangars on Ford Island.

PEARL CITY

# THE SECOND ATTACK WAVE
# PEARL HARBOR, 0850–0930 hrs

Tactically speaking the Japanese attack was a success: few proposed targets were missed. *Arizona* and *Oklahoma* were so badly mauled that they would never return to service. Japanese losses during the Second Wave amounted to 20 aircraft, eight of them claimed by anti-aircraft fire. A few ships did manage to get underway, but these were in the minority. Curiously, the fuel tank farms were not hit: the Japanese knew of them, but probably supposed that with the ships damaged, they were not worth the trouble. This proved to be a major mistake, as relaying fuel could have been a major obstacle to the US mounting a Pacific offensive.

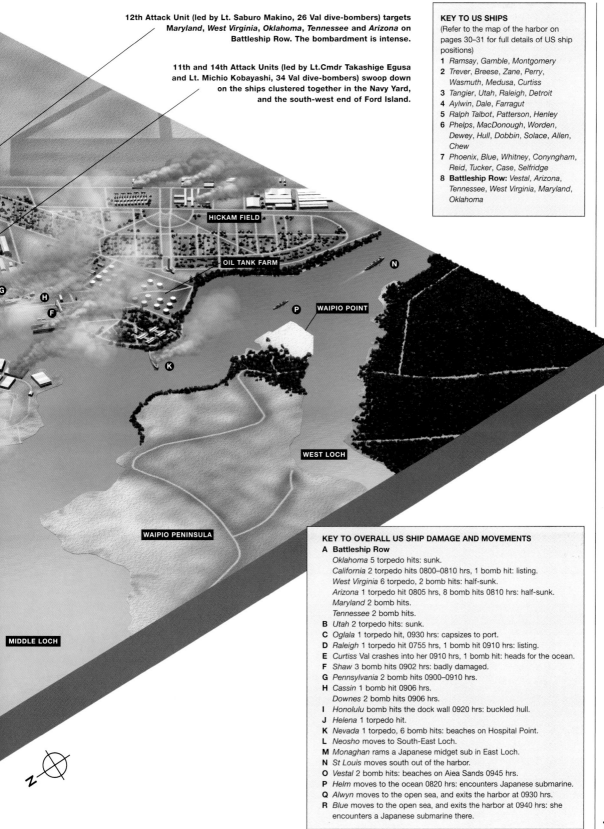

**12th Attack Unit** (led by Lt. Saburo Makino, 26 Val dive-bombers) targets *Maryland*, *West Virginia*, *Oklahoma*, *Tennessee* and *Arizona* on Battleship Row. The bombardment is intense.

**11th and 14th Attack Units** (led by Lt.Cmdr Takashige Egusa and Lt. Michio Kobayashi, 34 Val dive-bombers) swoop down on the ships clustered together in the Navy Yard, and the south-west end of Ford Island.

HICKAM FIELD

OIL TANK FARM

N

P WAIPIO POINT

G

H

F

K

WEST LOCH

WAIPIO PENINSULA

MIDDLE LOCH

Z

**KEY TO US SHIPS**
(Refer to the map of the harbor on pages 30–31 for full details of US ship positions)
1 *Ramsay, Gamble, Montgomery*
2 *Trever, Breese, Zane, Perry, Wasmuth, Medusa, Curtiss*
3 *Tangier, Utah, Raleigh, Detroit*
4 *Aylwin, Dale, Farragut*
5 *Ralph Talbot, Patterson, Henley*
6 *Phelps, MacDonough, Worden, Dewey, Hull, Dobbin, Solace, Allen, Chew*
7 *Phoenix, Blue, Whitney, Conyngham, Reid, Tucker, Case, Selfridge*
8 **Battleship Row:** *Vestal, Arizona, Tennessee, West Virginia, Maryland, Oklahoma*

**KEY TO OVERALL US SHIP DAMAGE AND MOVEMENTS**
**A Battleship Row**
  *Oklahoma* 5 torpedo hits: sunk.
  *California* 2 torpedo hits 0800–0810 hrs, 1 bomb hit: listing.
  *West Virginia* 6 torpedo, 2 bomb hits: half-sunk.
  *Arizona* 1 torpedo hit 0805 hrs, 8 bomb hits 0810 hrs: half-sunk.
  *Maryland* 2 bomb hits.
  *Tennessee* 2 bomb hits.
**B** *Utah* 2 torpedo hits: sunk.
**C** *Oglala* 1 torpedo hit, 0930 hrs: capsizes to port.
**D** *Raleigh* 1 torpedo hit 0755 hrs, 1 bomb hit 0910 hrs: listing.
**E** *Curtiss* Val crashes into her 0910 hrs, 1 bomb hit: heads for the ocean.
**F** *Shaw* 3 bomb hits 0902 hrs: badly damaged.
**G** *Pennsylvania* 2 bomb hits 0900–0910 hrs.
**H** *Cassin* 1 bomb hit 0906 hrs.
  *Downes* 2 bomb hits 0906 hrs.
**I** *Honolulu* bomb hits the dock wall 0920 hrs: buckled hull.
**J** *Helena* 1 torpedo hit.
**K** *Nevada* 1 torpedo, 6 bomb hits: beaches on Hospital Point.
**L** *Neosho* moves to South-East Loch.
**M** *Monaghan* rams a Japanese midget sub in East Loch.
**N** *St Louis* moves south out of the harbor.
**O** *Vestal* 2 bomb hits: beaches on Aiea Sands 0945 hrs.
**P** *Helm* moves to the ocean 0820 hrs: encounters Japanese submarine.
**Q** *Alwyn* moves to the open sea, and exits the harbor at 0930 hrs.
**R** *Blue* moves to the open sea, and exits the harbor at 0940 hrs: she encounters a Japanese submarine there.

## Japanese losses

Aircraft: nine fighters, 15 dive-bombers, five torpedo planes.
Submarines: one *I*-class sub, five midget subs.
Casualties: 55 airmen, 121 submarine crewmen, nine midget
   sub crewmen.

Before the oily smoke had drifted away, the United States was no longer neutral. After two hours of air strikes, the day of the battleship had passed as decisively as the day of horse cavalry. Air power, which had been tolerated and given lip service by many, became the branch of service of the hour.

The United States would have entered World War II eventually, but whether her entry would have been in time to aid Britain is open to discussion. Certainly she would have butted heads with Japan sooner or later. Had the great sea battle happened, many Japanese and American vessels would have gone to the bottom where no one could have recovered them, and the outcome of such a battle would have been inconclusive, for neither side was prepared for invasion. Had the American Navy waited and sortied, they would have lost carriers they could ill afford to lose much earlier than at Midway.

Yamamoto was correct in stating that the Japanese attack on Pearl Harbor awakened a sleeping giant, because it unified the American people (who were just recovering from the Depression) against a common enemy. While the atrocities and horrors of war were on European or Asian soil, Americans could ignore or lessen their impact, remaining officially uninvolved. Once American lives had been lost, they could no longer afford the luxury of neutrality or isolationism.

RIGHT **Although the Japanese suffered few casualties, not all pilots made it home safely. This Zero was shot down during the attack.**

The Japanese were right to assume that the United States was the greatest threat to their growth in the Pacific. The United States would eventually have entered World War II, but Pearl Harbor put the Americans on the fast track.

Payback was not long in coming, for the battle at Midway stopped the Japanese advance and curbed their naval superiority. Afterwards the road to Tokyo took three long years and was paved with the steel and blood of both sides.

Americans rallied around the icon of Pearl Harbor the way earlier generations had heeded the nationalistic imperative of 'Remember the Alamo'. The shame and anger they felt from the resounding defeat at Pearl Harbor could not be laid to rest until they had taken the war to Japanese soil.

In the gray days of fading sunlight of late December 1941, the Americans turned their eyes to Europe and Asia, mouths grimly set, and tightened their belts for war production and conscription. Conditions would get worse before they could improve. Bataan, Wake, the Philippines, Midway, Coral Sea, the Solomons and other names sent families to atlases to locate far-flung and exotic locations where loved ones flew, sailed or slogged through jungle.

The war with Japan ended on the deck of the USS *Missouri* at 0903 hrs on 2 September 1945 in Tokyo Bay, but it all began at 0753 hrs, 7 December 1941 at Pearl Harbor.

After the attack all troops were put on alert, and artillery deployed in prepared positions, as shown here. Rumor had it that invasion was at hand. However the invasion never materialized.

# FURTHER READING

*Jane's Fighting Ships of World War II,* Crescent Books, Avenel, NJ, 1995
(reprint)

Agawa, Hiroyuki (Trans. John Bester) *The Reluctant Admiral: Yamamoto and the Imperial Navy*, Kodansha International Ltd., Tokyo, 1979

Albright, Harry *Pearl Harbor: Japan's Fatal Blunder*, Hippocrene Books, New York, 1988

Bagnasco, Ermino *Submarines of World War II*, Naval Institute Press, Annapolis, MD, 1977

Barker, A.J. Col. (retired) *Pearl Harbor: Tora, Tora, Tora*, Ballantine Books, NY, 1988

Boatner, Mark M. III *The Biographical Dictionary of World War II,* Presidio Press, Novato, California, 1996

Breuer, William *Devil Boats: The PT War Against Japan,* Presidio Press, Novato, California, 1987

Carpenter, Dorr and Polmar, Norman *Submarines of the Imperial Japanese Navy*, Naval Institute Press, Annapolis, MD, 1996

Clausen, Henry C. and Bruce, Lee *Pearl Harbor: Final Judgment,* Crown Publishers, New York, 1992

Devereaux, James P.S. *The Story of Wake Island,* J.P. Lippincott Co., New York, 1947

Dull, Paul S. *A Battle History of the Imperial Japanese Navy (1941–1945),* Naval Institute Press, Annapolis, MD, 1978

Editors of Army Times, *A Military History: Pearl Harbor and Hawaii,* Bonanza Books, New York, 1971

Esposito, Vincent J. (Col. USA) *The West Point Atlas of American Wars, Vol. I*, Frederick A. Praeger Publishers, New York, 1959

Fahey, James C. *The Ships and Aircraft of the US Fleet (Fahey's Second War Edition)*, Gemsc Inc., New York, 1944

Forte, Robert S. and Marcello, Ronald E. *Remembering Pearl Harbor: Eyewitness Accounts by US Military Men and Women,* Scholarly Resources Imprint, Wilmington, DE, 1991

Fukodome, Shigeru (V.Adm. IJN, retired) *'Hawaii Operation'*, United States Naval Institute Proceedings, Annapolis, MD, 1955

Goldstein, Donald M. and Dillon, Katherine V. *The Pearl Harbor Papers: Inside The Japanese Plans,* Brassey's US, Mclean, VA, 1993

Green, William and Swanborough, Gordon *The Complete Book of Fighters*, Smithmark Books, New York, 1994

Hara, Tameichyi (Cpt. retired, IJN) Saito, Fred and Pineau, Roger *Japanese Destroyer Captain*, Ballantine Books, New York, 1961

Hata, Ikuhiko and Izawa, Yasuho (Trans. D.C. Gorham) *Japanese Naval Aces and Fighter Units in World War II*, Naval Institute Press, Annapolis, MD, 1989

Hoyt, Edwin P. *The Last Kamikaze: the Story of Admiral Matome Ugaki*, Praeger Publishers, Westport, CT, 1993

Ienaga, Saburo (Trans. Frank Baldwin) *The Pacific War 1931–1945*, Pantheon Books, New York, 1978

Kennedy, John S. *The Forgotten Warriors of Kaneohe*, East Bay Blue Print, Oakland, 1996 [Contact John S. Kennedy, 17271 Via Carmen, San Lorenzo, CA 94580-2611, USA, email: siddorken@aol.com, for all enquiries]

Keegan, John *The Second World War,* Penguin Books, New York, 1990

LaForte, Robert S. and Marcello, Ronald E. *Remembering Pearl Harbor: Eyewitness Accounts by US Military Men and Women,* SR Books, Wilmington, DE, 1991

Lord, Walter *Day of Infamy,* Bantam Books, New York, 1963

McCombs, Don and Worth, Fred L. *World War II: Strange & Fascinating Facts,* Greenwich House, New York, 1983

McIntyre, Donald (Cpt. retired) *Aircraft Carrier: The Majestic Weapon,* Ballantine Books, New York, 1971

Morisson, Samuel Eliot (Adm. USN, retired) *The Two Ocean War*, Ballantine Books, New York, 1963

Morrison, Wilbur H. *Above and Beyond 1941–1945,* Bantam Books, New York, 1983

Prange, Gordon W., Goldstein, Donald M. and Dillon, Katherine V. *At Dawn We Slept: The Untold Story of Pearl Harbor*, Penguin Books USA Inc., New York, 1982

Prange, Gordon W., Goldstein, Donald M. and Dillon, Katherine V. *Pearl Harbor: The Verdict of History,* Penguin Books USA Inc., New York, 1986

Prange, Gordon W., Donald M. Goldstein and Katherine V. Dillon, *Dec. 7 1941: The Day the Japanese Attacked Pearl Harbor,* Warner Books, New York, 1988

Reilly, John C. Jr *United States Navy Destroyers of World War II,* Blandford Press, Poole, Dorset, 1983

Smith, S.E. (Ed.) *The United States Navy in World War II,* Quill Books, William Morrow, New York, 1966

Smurthwaite, David *The Pacific War Atlas: 1941–1945, Facts on File,* New York, 1995

Toland, John *Infamy: Pearl Harbor and its Aftermath,* Berkeley Publishing, New York, 1983

Toland, John *But Not In Shame,* Ballantine Books, New York, 1961

Wallin, Homer N. (V.Adm.) *Pearl Harbor: Why, How, Fleet Salvage and Final Appraisal,* US Government Printing Office, Naval History Division, Washington D.C., 1968

Watts, Anthony J. *Japanese Warships of World War II,* Doubleday & Co., Garden City, NY, 1966

Weintraub, Stanley *Long Days Journey into War: December 7, 1941,* Truman Talley Books, New York, 1991

Young, Peter (Brig. retired) (Ed.) *The World Almanac Book of World War II,* Bison Books Ltd, London, 1981

Zich, Arthur *World War II: The Rising Sun,* Time-Life Books, Alexandria, VA, 1977

# WARGAMING PEARL HARBOR

**W**argaming Pearl Harbor is similar to gaming Custer's Last Stand, the Alamo, Borodino (as the French), Balaclava (as English Cavalry), or Appomattox (as the Confederates): the result is inevitable, and the intellectual pursuit in gaming it is not to see if one can win with the deck stacked, but to see relative to actual results how well one can do. To the best of my knowledge, there is no simulation board game currently available for Pearl Harbor.

The ideal game necessarily has three components:

1. A search and evasion segment.
2. A combat segment once the opposing commanders encounter one another.
3. An escape and pursuit (if the Americans locate the Japanese carrier force) segment.

Since the real battle involved the Japanese task force remaining hidden as it approached from the north, and the US carriers making a training sortie out of the harbor to the south of the island and delivering planes to Midway and Wake Island, it was by the merest coincidence that they could not locate each other. But what if the task forces had not done what historically they did?

The game could be set up with miniatures, as a paper game or as a combination of the two. Picture a map with Pearl Harbor in the middle

*Pennsylvania* was in dry dock, and because she was somewhat protected from both aerial and torpedo attacks, damage was less than on other battleships. This picture, taken a couple of years earlier, shows her six forward guns. Note the hospital ship and tug in the background off her port side.

of 12 concentric circles and surrounding areas superimposed with six pie-shaped segments whose apexes meet at Pearl Harbor (six 60° wedges). Each resulting piece of the pie goes out a distance of 12 areas, roughly 25 miles, for a total distance of 300 miles. As the approach area was barely 200 miles away, this allows the Japanese and American players ample room to maneuver.

The rules are simple: the Japanese have only the ships and carriers actually available. They may be advanced in the historic task force formation or in any reasonable formation the Japanese player desires. The Americans have a few restrictions, but they must have no less than one third of the American Pacific Fleet in the harbor at any time; up to two thirds of the fleet may be out (a third on maneuvers or returning and a third going out and relieving them). Ships in the harbor are stationary except those entering (having been relieved) or leaving (to relieve those at sea). Ships must rotate in some fashion every five days, except those in dry dock.

Each move represents a two-hour time period. There are 12 moves per day. American and Japanese ships may move one area every two hours. Air recon from Pearl Harbor may fly a scouting mission three times during a day, crossing through a total of six segments before returning to the air base (which is one of the six). These flights only occur during daylight hours (0600–1900). The American player may use radar twice daily (0400–0800) to inspect any two wedge parts not immediately adjacent to the island to account for the 'blocking' effect of the mountains.

There are three identical area maps and one battle board map – one for the Japanese player's hidden advance, one for the American player's ships on hidden maneuvers, and one which both may see. If any player uses searches to find the other player's fleet and finds the fleet, it is placed on the third map with the stationary pieces at Pearl Harbor for both sides to see. Ships in harbor or in a fleet which are attacked go on the battle board.

The Japanese aim is straightforward: to sink as many American carriers and battleships as possible without being discovered, and then return to safety by exiting the map towards Japan and preserving as many Japanese vessels and aircraft as possible. The American has two goals: first, to keep as many vessels as possible from harm, and second, to find the Japanese fleet once an attack occurs and sink the fleet.

Winners are determined by a simple point system. The Japanese player gets; one point for each US aircraft and vessel smaller than a destroyer or non-combatant ship; two points for each light cruiser; three points for heavy cruisers; four points for battleships; and five points for carriers. The Japanese get five points for a 'surprise' attack in which they approach the target without being spotted. The US gets similar points for Japanese vessels and five points if he locates and closes with the Japanese fleet.

The winner is the one with the most points accumulated when the Japanese player exits the area map board. The addictive part of such a battle is beating one's own previous best score, and it can be replayed until the activity becomes as much a mind game as chess.

# PEARL HARBOR TODAY

The bright sun reflects dazzlingly from blue waters surrounding the walkway, strong enough to give you a headache if you are not wearing sunglasses. Sound carries a great distance over water, and the roar of planes landing at the nearby international airport draw to mind the events which pulled the United States into World War II. All is peaceful, as Cmdr Fuchida noted over half a century ago. Today the American flag undulates on the sea breeze above the sunken remains of the USS *Arizona*. Contrary to urban legend, *Arizona* is not carried on the in-service roll.

## How to get there

If you don't want any hassle, consider taking a tour bus. Ask your hotel concierge or use the yellow pages to find the phone numbers of tour bus companies and call for scheduled Pearl Harbor tours.

Visitors to Oahu can either take the bus or rent a car to visit the site. Buses leave from several locations around Waikiki and offer a regular scheduled service. The No. 20 bus is your best bet since it offers a direct service, but the 47 bus also goes there. If in doubt, ask the hotel concierge for a bus route, a map, and advice on which bus to catch, where to transfer and so on. Other buses go past the Memorial bus stop at the Ala Moana shopping center. For schedules or details, call (808) 848 5555, the bus information number.

By car, take Kalia Road east. Go through Ft De Russey to Ala Moana Boulevard. Turn left onto Ala Moana Boulevard and follow it past the Ala

Troops manned listening posts, observation posts and machine-guns nests in preparation for repeat attacks or invasions following the early morning events of 7 December, but after the first two waves an uneventful stillness settled over Oahu.

After the attack Nagumo decided the Japanese had done well enough. The US feverishly labored to raise sunken ships. From top left to bottom right, the vessels are *California*, *Maryland* (afloat), *Oklahoma* (capsized), *Tennessee*, *West Virginia* and *Arizona*. The oil slick is primarily from *Arizona*.

Moana shopping center. Once past the shopping center, this road merges with Nimitz Highway (Highway 92) and changes to that name. Stay on Nimitz past all the Honolulu airport exits until you reach Kamehameha Highway (Highway 99) which is past the airport. Bear right to enter Kamehameha Highway. Follow it past the Navy Halawa Gate and housing area. You will see signs for the Pearl Harbor Visitor Center, which is on your left, and visitor parking is available.

### The Visitor Center

The Visitor Center was dedicated in 1962 and became a part of the National Park Service System in 1980. Over one and a half million visitors come through this park each year. As Hawaii is a tropical island, wear sunscreen and light clothing, and take a light waterproof jacket or umbrella for afternoon showers.

The USS *Arizona* Visitor Center lies within the Pearl Harbor Naval Base and is a monument now operated and maintained by the National Park Service through an arrangement with the United States Navy. The park consists of a visitor center, theater, museum, bookshop and waterfront exhibits. Nearby is the USS *Bowfin* submarine exhibit and park. The *Arizona* Monument floats above the sunken remains of the

USS *Arizona* and the honored seamen who rest within her rusting bosom. A flag is raised and lowered over the memorial each day.

As a National Park Service site, the *Arizona* Memorial is open daily from 0730 hrs to 1700 hrs year round except on special holidays (Thanksgiving, Christmas Day and New Year's Day). Special programs run on 7 December and Memorial Day. Although admission is free, donations to help defray costs of upkeep are encouraged.

Tourists arriving at the center are issued tickets. This is to ensure that everyone who wants to see the memorial can do so in an orderly manner. Tours are on a first come, first served basis – you cannot make reservations. At the center a 23-minute film produced by the National Park Service gives visitors an overview of the history and events leading up to the Japanese attack on the US warships at Pearl Harbor.

After viewing the film, visitors catch a shuttle boat out to the memorial. The total program takes about one hour and 15 minutes. Tours begin at 0800 hrs. There is usually a short wait because the memorial is one of the best-known tourist meccas in Hawaii, and waits of up to an hour are not uncommon. Usually it is best to schedule this as the first event of the day because of this. The last program of the day begins at 1500 hrs.

### Information
The monument address is: USS *Arizona* Memorial, 1 Arizona Memorial Place, Honolulu, HA 96818-3145, telephone (808) 422 2771 or (808) 422 0561 for recorded messages.

Take your camera, sunscreen and plenty of film to record the quiet, seaborne tranquillity of one of Oahu's most-visited historic locations.

**Sunset at Schofield Barracks. The military waited for the other shoe to drop, but contrary to military expectations, there was no follow-up attack, even though the US was now at war.**

# APPENDICES

| Name | ID No. | Notes | Guns | Speed | Year | TT | AC | Disp | AB | Crew |
|------|--------|-------|------|-------|------|----|----|------|-----|------|
| **Enterprise** + | CV6 | Flagship of TF8-VADM Halsey.Taking F43's to Wake | 8-5"38AA; 16-1.1MG; | 34.0 | 1936 | 0 | (85) 18 F4F 36 SBD 18 TBD 2 VT6 | 19.9 | B4 | 2,072 |
| **Lexington** + | CV2 | Task Force 12 Taking SB2U3's to Midway | 8-8".55; 12-5".25; 4-6pdr | 33.9 | 1927 | 0 | (81) 19 F2A 32 SBD 12 VT2 PLUS 18 SB2U | 33.0 | B6; D3 | 1,899 |
| **Saratoga** + | CV3 | Refitting in San Diego | 8-8".55; 12-5".25; 4-6pdr | 33.9 | 1928 | 0 | 81 | 33.0 | B6;D3 | 1,899 |
| **California** | BB44 | PH | 12-14"/50; 16-5".38; 40mm | 21.0 | 1919 | 0 | (4) 2 OSU2-3 | 32.6 | B14; T9-18; D2.5-3.5 | 2,200 |
| **Maryland** | BB46 | PH | 8-16"/45; 8-5"/.38; 10-5"/.51; | 30.0 | 1920 | 0 | (3) None | 31.5 | B16; T9-18; D3 | 2,100 |
| **Oklahoma** | BB37 | PH | 10-14"/45; 12-5".51; 12-5".25; 4-6pdr;8MG | 20.5 | 1914 | 0 | (3) None | 29.0 | B8-13.5; D2-5; T9-18 | 1,301 |
| **Tennessee** | BB43 | PH | 12-14"/50; 16-5".38 40mm | 21.0 | 1919 | 0 | (3) 3 OSU2-3 | 32.3 | B14; D3; 9-18 T9-18 | 2,200 |
| **West Virginia** | BB48 | PH | 8-16"/45; 16-5".38 10-5".51 | 30.0 | 1921 | 0 | (3) 1 OSU2-3 | 31.8 | B14-16; T9-18; D3 | 2,350 |
| **Arizona** | BB39 | PH | 12-14"/45; 12-5".51; {12}-5".38 | 21.0 | 1915 | 0 | (3) 2 OSU2-3 | 32.6 | B8-14; D3-6; T9-18 | 1,500 |
| **Pennsylvania** | BB38 | PH | 12-14"/45; 12-5".51; 12-5".25; 4-3pdr | 21.0 | 1915 | 0 | (3) 1 OS2U1 3 OS2U3 | 33.1 | B8-14; D2-6; T9-18 | 1,358 |
| **Nevada** | BB36 | PH | 10-14"/45; 12-5.51; 12-5".25; 4-6pdr; 8MG | 21.0 | 1914 | 0 | (3) None | 29.0 | B8-13.5; D2-5' T9-18 | 1,301 |
| **Colorado** + | BB45 | At Puget Sound | 8-16"; 8-5"/.38; 10-5".51 | 21.0 | 1916 | 0 | 3 | 32.5 | B16; T9-18; D3 | (1,500) |
| **Helena** | CL50 | PH | 9-8".55; 12-5".38; 44-40mm 22-28 20mm | 32.5 | 1938 | 0 | (4) 3 SOC3 1 SON1 | 13.6 | S6-8; D3+2 | 1,700 |
| **Minneapolis** + | CA36 | 25 miles S of Oahu | 9-8"/5.5; 8-5"/.25; 16-40mm; 19-20mm | 32.7 | 1934 | 0 | 4 SOC1 | 9.95 | S1.5-5; D3+2; T3-6 | 876-1,200 |
| **Portland** + | CA33 | W/CV2 | 9-8"/5.5; 8-5"/.25; 24-40mm; 16-20mm | 32.7 | 1933 | 0 | 4 3 SOC1 1 SOC2 | 9.8 | S3-4; D2+2; T1.5-3 | 876-1,200 |
| **Salt Lake City** + | CA24 | W/CV6 | 10-8"/.55, 4-5"/25 | 32.7 | 1929 | 0 | 4 SOC1 | 9.1 | S-3 D2+1 | 700 |
| **Chester** + | CA27 | W/CV6 | 9-8"/55, 12-5"/38 | 32.7 | 1929 | 0 | 4 2 SOC1 2 SOC2 | 9.05 | | 700 |
| **Northamton** + | CA26 | RADM Spruance W/CV6 | 9-8"/55, 12-5"/38 | 32.7 | 1930 | 0 | 4 SOC1 | 9.05 S-3 D2+1 | | 700 |
| **New Orleans** + | CA32 | PH | 9-8"/5.5; 8-5"/.25; 16-40mm; 19-20mm | 32.7 | 1933 | 0 | 4 2 SOC1 2 SOC2 | 9.95 | S1.5-5; D3+2; T3-6 | 876-1,200 |
| **San Francisco** | CA38 | PH | 9-8"/5.5; 8-5"/.25; 16-40mm; 19-20mm | 32.7 | 1933 | 0 | 4 (5) 2 SOC1 3 SOC2 | 9.95 | S1.5-5; D3+2; T3-6 | 876-1,200 |

| Name | ID No. | Notes | Guns | Speed | Year | TT | AC | Disp | AB | Crew |
|------|--------|-------|------|-------|------|-----|-----|------|-----|-------|
| Honolulu | CL48 | PH | 15-6".47; 8-5"/.25; 16-40mm; 24-20mm 2-3pdr; 8MG | 32.5 | 1937 | 6-21 | 0 (4) 3 SOC3 1 SON1 | 10.0 | D1.5; S3 | 458 |
| Pensacola + | CA24 | Escort duty/ Somoa | 10/8" 55, 4/5" 25 | 32.7 | 1929 | 0 | 4 SOC1 | 9.1 | S3,D2+1, T1.5 | 700 |
| Chicago + | CA29 | W/CV2 | 9-8".55 8-5" 25 | 32.7 | 1928 | 0 | 5 (4) 1 SOC1 3 SOC2 | 9.3 | S3,D2+1, T1.5 | 872-1,200 |
| Indianapolis + | CA35 | W/TF3 off Johnson Island | 9-8" 55, 8-5" .25; 24-40mm 16-20mm | 32.7 | 1931 | 0 | 4 SOC1 | 9.8 | S1.5-5, D3+2; T5-6 & T3; Twr8 | 876-1,200 |
| Astoria + | CA34 | W/CV2 | 9-8".55 8-5".25; 16-40mm 19-20mm | 32.7 | 1933 | 0 | 4 SOC1 | 9.95 | S1.5-6, D3+2; T5-6 & T3; CT8 | 876-1,200 |
| Louisville + | CA28 | Escort duty in Solomon Islands | 9-8" 55; 8-5" 25; 32-40mm 27-20mm | 32.7 | 1931 | 0 | 3 SOC1 1 SOC2 | 9.05 | S3;D2+1; T1.5 | 876-1,200 |
| St Louis + | CL49 | PH | 15-6" .47; 8-5" .38; 16-40mm 24-20mm | 32.5 | 1938 | 0 | 4 32 SOC3 1 SON1 | 9.7 | S1-1-5; D3+2; T3-5 | 888 |
| Raleigh | CL7 | PH | 10-6" .53; 8-3" .50; 2-3pdr; 8MG | 35.0 | 1922 | 6-21 | 2 (3) 2 SOC3 1 SON1 | 7.05 | S3; D1.5; | 458 |
| Detroit | CL8 | PH | 10-6" .53; 8-3" .50; 2-3pdr; 8MG | 35.0 | 1922 | 6-21 | 2 (1) 1 SOC3 | 7.05 | S3; D1.5; | 458 |
| Phoenix | CL46 | PH | 15-6" .47; 8-5" .25; 16-40mm; 24-20mm | 32.5 | 1938 | 0 | 2 (1) 4 SOC3 | 9.7 | S1.5-5; D1.5; D3+2 T3-5 | 975–1,200 |
| Jarvis | DD393 | PH | 4-5"/38 | 36.5 | 1934 | 5-21" | 0 | 1.63 | {} | 210 |
| Mugford | DD389 | PH | 4-5"/38 | 36.5 | 1934 | 5-21" | 0 | 1.63 | {} | 210 |
| Cummings | DD365 | PH | 4-5".38 | 36.5 | 1937 | 12-21" | 0 | 1.46 | {} | 158 |
| Schley | DD103 | PH | 6-3"/DPA; 2MG | 35.0 | 1918 | 6-21" | 0 | 1.06 | {} | {122} |
| Bagley | DD386 | PH | 4-5"/38 | 36.5 | 1938 | 5-21" | 0 | 1.63 | {} | 210 |
| Hopkins + | DMS13 | w/TF3 | 4-4" | 35.0 | 1917 | 12-21" | 0 | 1.09 | {} | 122 |
| Southard + | DMS10 | w/TF3 | 4-4" 50 | 35.0 | 1918 | 12-21" | 0 | 1.19 | {} | 122 |
| Dorsey + | DMS1 | w/TF3 | 4-4" 50 | 35.0 | 1918 | 12-21" | 0 | 1.09 | {} | 122 |
| Elliot + | DMS4 | w/TF3 | 4-4" 50 | 35.0 | 1917 | 12-21" | 0 | 1.09 | {} | 122 |
| Long + | DMS12 | w/TF3 | 4-4" 50 | 35.0 | 1918 | 12-21" | 0 | 1.19 | {} | 122 |
| Hull | DD350 | PH | 4-5".38 | 36.5 | 1935 | 8-21" | 0 | 1.39 | {} | {162} |
| Chandler + | DMS9 | w/CA36 25 miles S of Oahu | 6-3"DPA, 2MG AA | 35.0 | 1919 | 6-21" | 0 | 1.1 | {} | 122 |
| Hovey + | DMS11 | w/CA36 | 4-4" 50 | 35.0 | 1918 | 12-21" | 0 | 1.19 | {} | 122 |
| Boggs + | DMS3 | w/CA36 | 4-4" 50 | 35.0 | 1917 | 12-21" | 0 | 1.09 | {} | 122 |
| Lamaberton + | DMS2 | w/CA36 | 4-4" 50 | 35.0 | 1917 | 12-21" | 0 | 1.09 | {} | 122 |
| Conyngham | DD371 | PH | 5-5"/38 20&40mmAA | 36.5 | 1936 | 12-21" | 0 | 1.5 | {} | 172 |
| McCall + | DD400 | w/CV6 | 4-5"/38, 20&40mmAA | 36.5 | 1935 | 16-21" | 0 | 1.5 | {} | 200 |
| Ellet + | DD398 | w/CV6 | 4-5"/38, 20&40mmAA | 36.5 | 1935 | 16-21" | 0 | 1.5 | {} | 200 |

| Name | ID No. | Notes | Guns | Speed | Year | TT | AC | Disp | AB | Crew |
|------|--------|-------|------|-------|------|-----|-----|------|-----|------|
| Benham + | DD397 | w/CV6 | 4-5"/38, 20&40mmAA | 36.5 | 1935 | 16-21" | 0 | 1.5 | {} | 200 |
| Craven + | DD382 | w/CV6 | 4-5"/38, 20&40mmAA | 36.5 | 1937 | 16-21" | 0 | 1.5 | {} | 200 |
| Dunlap + | DD384 | w/CV6 | 5-5"/38, 20&40mmAA | 36.5 | 1937 | 12-21" | 0 | 1.5 | {} | 172 |
| Fanning + | DD385 | w/CV6 | 5-5"/38, 20&40mmAA | 36.5 | 1937 | 12-21" | 0 | 1.5 | {} | 172 |
| Balch + | DD363 | w/CV6 | 8-5"/38, 20&40mmAA | 37.0 | 1936 | 8-21" | 0 | 1.8 | {} | 230 |
| Maury + | DD401 | w/CV6 | 4-5"/38, 20&40mmAA | 36.5 | 1935 | 16-21" | 0 | 1.5 | {} | 200 |
| MacDonough | DD351 | PH | 4-5"/38 | 36.5 | 1935 | 8-21" | 0 | 1.39 | {} | {162} |
| Worden | DD352 | PH | 4-5"/38 | 36.5 | 1934 | 8-21" | 0 | 1.41 | {} | {162} |
| Dewey | DD349 | PH | 4-5"/38 | 36.5 | 1934 | 8-21" | 0 | 1.34 | {} | {162} |
| Phelps | DD360 | PH | 6-5".38; 6-40mm | 37.0 | 1936 | 8-21" | 0 | 1.80 | {} | 230 |
| Allen | DD66 | PH | 3-4".50; 3-3"AA | 29.5 | 1916 | 6-21" | 0 | .92 | {} | 136 |
| Chew | DD106 | PH | 6-3"DPA; 2MG | 35.0 | 1918 | 6-21" | 0 | 1.06 | {} | 122 |
| Henley | DD391 | PH | 4-5".38 | 36.5 | 1937 | 16-21" | 0 | 1.5 | {} | 200 |
| Blue | DD387 | PH | 4-5".38 | 36.5 | 1937 | 16-21" | 0 | 1.5 | {} | 200 |
| Helm | DD388 | PH | 4-5".38 | 36.5 | 1937 | 16-21" | 0 | 1.5 | {} | 200 |
| Reid | DD369 | PH | 4-5".38 | 36.5 | 1937 | 12-21" | 0 | 1.48 | {} | 172 |
| Tucker | DD374 | PH | 4-5".38 | 36.5 | 1936 | 12-21" | 0 | 1.5 | {} | 172 |
| Case | DD370 | PH | 4-5".38 | 36.5 | 1935 | 12-21" | 0 | 1.5 | {} | 172 |
| Porter + | DD356 | w/CV2 | 8-5" 38 | 37.0 | 1936 | 8-21" | 0 | 1.8 | {} | 162 |
| Drayton + | DD366 | w/CV2 | 5-5" 38 | 36.5 | 1933 | 8-21" | 0 | 1.5 | {} | 230 |
| Flusser + | DD368 | w/CV2 | 5-5" 38 | 36.5 | 1933 | 8-21" | 0 | 1.5 | {} | 230 |
| Lamson + | DD367 | w/CV2 | 5-5" 38 | 36.5 | 1933 | 8-21" | 0 | 1.5 | {} | 230 |
| Mahan + | DD364 | w/CV2 | 5-5" 38 | 36.5 | 1933 | 8-21" | 0 | 1.5 | {} | 230 |
| Gridley + | DD380 | w/CV6 | 4-5".38 | 36.5 | 1936 | 16-21" | 0 | 1.5 | {} | 200 |
| Selfridge | DD357 | PH | 6-5".38; 6-40mm | 37.0 | 1937 | 8-21" | 0 | 1.85 | {} | 230 |
| Patterson | DD392 | PH | 4-5".38 DPA | 36.5 | 1938 | 16-21" | 0 | 1.5 | {} | 200 |
| Ralph Talbot | DD390 | PH | 4-5".38 DPA | 36.5 | 1938 | 16-21" | 0 | 1.5 | {} | 200 |
| Monaghan | DD354 | PH | 4-5".38 | 36.5 | 1933 | 8-21" | 0 | 1.39 | {} | 162 |
| Farragut | DD348 | PH | 4-5".38 | 36.5 | 1934 | 8-21" | 0 | 1.36 | {} | 162 |
| Dale | DD353 | PH | 4-5".38 | 36.5 | 1935 | 8-21" | 0 | 1.39 | {} | 162 |
| Aylwin | DD355 | PH | 4-5". 38 | 36.5 | 1935 | 8-21" | 0 | 1.37 | {} | 162 |
| Litchfield + | DD336 | 60 miles SW of Oahu | 6-3"DPA; 2mg | 35.0 | 1920 | 6-21" | 0 | 1.19 | {} | 122 |
| Cassin | DD372 | PH | 4-5.38" | 36.5 | 1933 | 12-21" | 0 | 1.5 | {} | 172 |
| Downes | DD375 | PH | 4-5"/38 | 36.5 | 1933 | 12-21" | 0 | 1.5 | {} | 172 |
| Ward (ex Cowell) | DD139 | PH | 6-3"DPA | 35.0 | 1918 | 6-21" | 0 | 1.06 | {} | 122 |
| Shaw | DD373 | PH | 4-5".38 | 36.5 | 1935 | 12-21" | 0 | 1.5 | {} | 172 |
| Thresher | SS200 | 60 miles SW of Oahu | 1-4" 2-20MM | 21.0 9.0 | 1938 | 10-21" 24 | 0 | 1.47 | {} | 80–85 |
| Oglala | CM4 | PH | 1-5".51 | 20.0 | 1917 | 0 | 0 | 4.2 | {} | 300 |
| Tracy | DM19 | PH | 4-4".50 | 35.0 | 1937* | 80M | 0 | 1.19 | {} | 122 |

| Name | ID No. | Notes | Guns | Speed | Year | TT | AC | | Disp | AB | Crew |
|------|--------|-------|------|-------|------|-----|-----|---|------|-----|------|
| Preble | DM20 | PH | 4-4".50 | 35.0 | 1937* | 80M | 0 | | 1.19 | {} | 122 |
| Pruitt | DM22 | PH | 4-4".50 | 35.0 | 1937* | 80M | 0 | | 1.19 | {} | 122 |
| Sicard | DM21 | PH | 4-4".50 | 35.0 | 1937* | 80M | 0 | | 1.19 | {} | 122 |
| Grebe | YMS43 | PH | 2-3".50AA | 14.0 | 1919 | 0 | 0 | | .26 | {} | 72 |
| Ramsay | DM16 | PH | 4-4".50 | 35.0 | 1930 | 80M | 0 | | 1.19 | {} | 122 |
| Breese | DM18 | PH | 4-4".50 | 35.0 | 1931 | 80M | 0 | | 1.19 | {} | 122 |
| Montgomery | DM17 | PH | 4-4".50 | 35.0 | 1931 | 80M | 0 | | 1.19 | {} | 122 |
| Gamble | DM15 | PH | 4-4".50 | 35.0 | 1931 | 80M | 0 | | 1.19 | {} | 122 |
| Zane | DMS14 | PH | 4-4".50 | 35.0 | 1940 | 80M | 0 | | 1.19 | {} | 122 |
| Trever | DMS16 | PH | 4-4".50 | 35.0 | 1940 | 80M | 0 | | 1.19 | {} | 122 |
| Perry | DMS17 | PH | 4-4".50 | 35.0 | 1940 | 80M | 0 | | 1.19 | {} | 122 |
| Wasmuth | DMS15 | PH | 4-4".50 | 35.0 | 1940 | 80M | 0 | | 1.19 | {} | 122 |
| Vireo | YMS52 | PH | 2-3".50AA | 14.0 | 1919 | 0 | 0 | | .84 | {} | 72 |
| Turkey | YMS13 | PH | 2-3".50AA | 14.0 | 1918 | 0 | 0 | | .84 | {} | 85 |
| Bobolink | YMS20 | PH | 2-3".50AA | 14.0 | 1919 | 0 | 0 | | .84 | {} | 72 |
| Rail | YMS26 | PH | 2-3".50AA | 14.0 | 1918 | 0 | 0 | | .84 | {} | 72 |
| Cockatoo (Vashon) | AMc8 | PH | 1-3"DPA | 14.0 | 1936 | 0 | 0 | | 1.31 | {} | 72 |
| Condor | AMc14 | PH | 1-3"DPA | 14.0 | 1937 | 0 | 0 | | .98 | {} | 72 |
| Reedbird | AMc30 | PH | 1-3"DPA | 14.0 | 1935 | 0 | 0 | | 1.27 | {} | 72 |
| Tern | YMS31 | PH | 2-3".50AA | 14.0 | 1919 | 0 | 0 | | .84 | {} | 72 |
| Crossbill | AMc9 | PH | 1-3"DPA | 14.0 | 1937 | 0 | 0 | | 1.15 | {} | 72 |
| Tautog | SS199 | PH | 1-4" 2-20MM | 21.0 9.0 | 1940 | 10-21"/24 | 0 | | 1.47 | {} | 65 |
| Plunger + | SS179 | 200 miles E of Oahu | 1-4" 2-20mm | 20.0 9.0 | 1934 | 6-21"/ | 0 | | 1.33 | {} | 57 |
| Pollack + | SS180 | 200 miles E of Oahu | 1-4" 2-20mm | 20.0 9.0 | 1934 | 6-21"/ | 0 | | 1.33 | {} | 57 |
| Pompano + | SS181 | 200 miles E of Oahu | 1-4" 2-20mm | 20.0 9.0 | 1934 | 6-21"/ | 0 | | 1.33 | {} | 57 |
| Gudgeon | SS211 | PH | 1-4" 2-20mm | 21.0 9.0 | 1941 | 10-21"/24 | 0 | | 1.47 | {} | 65 |
| Tambour + | SS198 | Near Wake | 1-3" 2-20mm | 20.0 9.0 | 1941 | 10-21"/24 | 0 | | 1.52 | {} | 65 |
| Triton + | SS201 | Near Wake | 1-3" 50 | 20.0 9.0 | 1941 | 10-21"/24 | 0 | | 1.52 | {} | 65 |
| Trout + | SS202 | Off Midway | 1-3" 2-20mm | 20.0 9.0 | 1941 | 10-21"/24 | 0 | | 1.52 | {} | 65 |
| Narwhal | SS167 | PH | 2-6" 4-20MM | 20.0 8.5 | 1930 | 10-21"/20 | 0 | | 2.73 | {} | 90 |
| Dolphin | SS169 | PH | 1-4.50 | 17.0 8.0 | 1932 | 6-21"/18 | 0 | | 1.54 | {} | 64 |
| Cachalot | SS170 | PH | 1-3"AA | 17.0 9.0 | 1933 | 6-21" | 0 | | 1.11 | {} | 52 |
| Widgeon | ASR1 | Sub Rescue | 2-3.50AA | 14.0 | 1918 | 0 | 0 | | 1.06 | {} | 79 |
| PT-20 | PT20 | PH | 4-.50NG | 41.0 | 1940 | 4-18" | 0 | | .35 | {} | 10 |
| PT-21 | PT21 | PH | 2-20mm | 41.0 | 1941 | 4-21" | 0 | | .51 | {} | 11 |
| PT-22 | PT22 | PH | 2-20mm | 41.0 | 1941 | 4-21" | 0 | | .51 | {} | 11 |
| PT-23 | PT23 | PH | 2-20mm | 41.0 | 1941 | 4-21" | 0 | | .51 | {} | 11 |
| PT-24 | PT24 | PH | 2-20mm | 41.0 | 1941 | 4-21" | 0 | | .51 | {} | 11 |
| PT-25 | PT25 | PH | 2-20mm | 41.0 | 1941 | 4-21" | 0 | | .51 | {} | 11 |

| Name | ID No. | Notes | Guns | Speed | Year | TT | AC | Disp | AB | Crew |
|------|--------|-------|------|-------|------|-----|-----|------|-----|-------|
| PT-26 | PT26 | PH | 2-20mm | 41.0 | 1941 | 4-21" | 0 | .51 | {} | 11 |
| PT-27 | PT27 | PH | 2-20mm | 41.0 | 1941 | 4-21" | 0 | .51 | {} | 11 |
| PT-28 | PT28 | PH | 2-20mm | 41.0 | 1941 | 4-21" | 0 | .51 | {} | 11 |
| PT-29 | PT29 | PH | 2-20mm | 41.0 | 1941 | 4-21" | 0 | .51 | {} | 11 |
| PT-30 | PT30 | PH | 2-20mm | 41.0 | 1941 | 4-21" | 0 | .51 | {} | 11 |
| PT-42 | PT42 | PH | 2-20mm | 41.0 | 1941 | 4-21" | 0 | .51 | {} | 11 |
| Argonnes | AG31 | PH Base force flagship sub tender | 1-3" | 15.5 | 1921 | 0 | 0 | 11.1 | {} | 85 |
| Wm. Ward Burroughs + | AP6 | Transport: en route to Wake Island | 4-3" 5MG | 14.0 | 1929 | 0 | 0 | 4.57 | {} | 178 |
| Casco + | AVP12 | w/BB45 | 4-5" 38; 5-40mm; | 18.0 | 1939 | 0 | 0 | 1.69 | {} | 215 |
| Williamson + | AVD2 | w/BB45 | 2-4"; | 25.0 | 1917 | 0 | 0 | 1.19 | () | 122 |
| Clark + | DD361 | Mare Island | 8-5" 38; | 37.0 | 1936 | 8-21" | 0 | 1.80 | {} | 230 |
| Cushing + | DD376 | Mare Island | 5-5" 38 | 36.5 | 1936 | 12-21" | 0 | 1.50 | () | 172 |
| Perkins + | DD377 | Mare Island | 5-5" 38 | 36.5 | 1936 | 12-21" | 0 | 1.50 | () | 172 |
| Preston + | DD379 | Mare Island | 5-5" 38 | 36.6 | 1936 | 12-21" | 0 | 1.50 | () | 172 |
| Smith + | DD378 | Mare Island | 5-5" 38 | 36.6 | 1936 | 12-21" | 0 | 1.50 | () | 172 |
| Rathburn + | DD113 | Mare Island | 4-4" 50 | 35.9 | 1918 | 12-21" | 0 | 1.09 | {} | 122 |
| SS27 + | SS132 | Mare Island | 1-4" 50 | 14.5 11.0 | 1924 | 4-21" | 0 | .80 | {} | 45 |
| SS28 + | SS133 | Mare Island | 1-4" 50 | 14.5 11.0 | 1922 | 4-21" | 0 | .80 | {} | 45 |
| Nautilus + | SS168 | Mare Island | 2-6" | 17.0 8.5 | 1924 | 6-21" | 0 | 2.73 | {} | 90 |
| Cuttlefish + | SS171 | Mare Island | 1-3" | 17.0 8.0 | 1934 | 6-21" | 0 | 1.10 | {} | 52 |
| Tuna + | SS203 | Mare Island | 1-3" | 20.0 9.0 | 1941 | 10-21" | 0 | 1.52 | {} | 65 |
| Kanawha + | AO1 | Mare Island | 1-5"; 4-4" | 14.0 | 1915 | 0 | 0 | 14.5 | {} | 150 |
| Sabine + | AO25 | Mare Island | 1-5";4-3" | 18.0 | 1940 | 0 | 0 | 18.35 | {} | 64 |
| Kaskaskia + | AO27 | Mare Island | 1-5"; 4-3" | 18.0 | 1940 | 0 | 0 | 23.23 | {} | 64 |
| Pelican + | AV6 | Mare Island | 1-5"; 2-3" | 14.0 | 1919 | 0 | 0 | .84 | {} | 85 |
| Bridge + | AF1 | Mare Island | (1-5"; 4-3") | 14.0 | 1914 | 0 | 0 | 8.5 | {} | (250) |
| Dixie + | AD14 | Mare Island | 4-5" 38; 8-40MM | 19.0 | 1939 | 0 | 0 | 14.03 | {} | 1,262 |
| Ballard + | AVD10 | En route to Mare Island | 2-4" | 25.0 | 1920 | 0 | 0 | 1.19 | {} | (122) |
| Teal + | AVP5 | Seattle | 2-3" | 14.0 | 1919 | 0 | 0 | .84 | {} | 85 |
| Concord + | CL10 | w/CV3 | 12-6" 53cal; 8-3"; 2-3lb; 8-MGAA | 20.0 | 1921 | 6-21" | 2 1 SOC3 1 SON1 | 7.05 | S3; UD1.5 | 458 |
| Dent + | DD116 | w/CV3 | 4-4" 50 | 35.0 | 1918 | 12-21" | 0 | 1.09 | {} | 122 |
| Talbot + | DD114 | w/CV3 | 4-4" 50 | 35.0 | 1918 | 12-21" | 0 | 1.09 | {} | 122 |
| Waters + | DD115 | w/CV3 | 4-4" 50 | 35.0 | 1918 | 12-21" | 0 | 1.09 | {} | 122 |
| SS18 | SS123 | w/CV3 | 1-4" 50 | 14.5 11.0 | 1920 | 4-21" | 0 | .80 | () | 45 |
| SS23 | SS128 | w/CV3 | 1-4" 50 | 14.5 11.0 | 1923 | 4-21" | 0 | .80 | () | 45 |
| SS34 | SS139 | w/CV3 | 1-4" 50 | 14.5 11.0 | 1923 | 4-21" | 0 | .80 | {} | 45 |
| SS35 | SS140 | w/CV3 | 1-4" 50 | 14.5 11.0 | 1923 | 4-21" | 0 | .80 | {} | 45 |
| Harris + | AP8 | w/CV3 | 4-3" | 18.0 | 1921 | 0 | 0 | 14.11 | {} | 628 |

| Name | ID No. | Notes | Guns | Speed | Year | TT | AC | Disp | AB | Crew |
|------|--------|-------|------|-------|------|----|----|------|----|----|
| Ortolan + | ASR5 | w/CV3 | 2-3" 50 | 14.0 | 1919 | 0 | 0 | 1.06 | {} | 79 |
| Cuyama + | AO3 | w/CV3 | 4-5" | 14.0 | 1915 | 0 | 0 | 14.5 | {} | (144) |
| Kaula + | AG33 | Ferry: en route 60 miles NE of Palmyra | 1-4" 2-3" | 12.0 | 1941 | 0 | 0 | 2.1 | {} | 70 |
| Kingfisher + | AM25 | Minesweeper near Samoa | 2-3" 50 | 14.0 | 1918 | 0 | 0 | .84 | {} | 72 |
| Sacramento | PG19 | Gunboat | 3-4".50 8MG | 12.5 | 1914 | 0 | 0 | 1.14 | {} | 172 |
| Keosanqua | AT38 | Fleet ocean tug | 2-3".50 | 13.0 | 1920 | 0 | 0 | .79 | {} | 51 |
| Seminole + | AT65 | Fleet ocean tug: Honolulu to San Diego | 1-3" | 16.2 | 1940 | 0 | 0 | 1.45 | {} | 55 |
| Arctic + | AF7 | At Lahaina | 1.5" | 11.0 | 1919 | 0 | 0 | 12.6 | {} | 211 |
| Sonoma + | AT12 | Between Oahu and Wake Island | 1-3" | 13.0 | 1912 | 0 | 0 | 14.0 | {} | (51) |
| Antares + | AKS3 | Honolulu: target repair ship | (4-5") | 15.0 | 1912 | 0 | 0 | (7.7) | {} | 197 |
| Vega + | AK17 | Honolulu: cargo ship | 2-5" | 11.5 | 1919 | 0 | 0 | 11.45 | {} | 227 |
| Seagull + | AM30 | Honolulu | 1-3" | 14.0 | 1919 | 0 | 0 | .84 | {} | 72 |
| Navaho (Navajo) | AT40 | Ocean-going tug | 1-3" | 16.5 | 1940 | 0 | 0 | 1.45 | {} | 55 |
| McFarland | AVD14 | PH Seaplane tender | 4-4" 1-3" | 25.0 | 1917 | 0 | 0 | 1.19 | {} | 122 |
| Sepulga + | AO20 | Near San Diego | (1-5"; 4-3") | 10.5 | 1920 | 0 | 0 | 16.8 | {} | 79 |
| Pinola + | AT33 | At San Pedro | 2-3" 50 | 13.0 | 1920 | 0 | 0 | 1.03 | {} | 51 |
| Platte + | AO24 | Los Angeles | 1-5"; 4-3" 8-40mm | 18.8 | 1939 | 0 | 0 | 18.3 | {} | 64 |
| Procyon + | AK19 | Alameda | 1-5" | 15.5 | 1940 | 0 | 0 | 9.27 | {} | 412 |
| Boreas + | AF9 | San Francisco | (1-5") | 11.0 | 1919 | 0 | 0 | 12.6 | {} | (275) |
| Aldebaran + | AF10 | San Francisco | 1-5"; 4-3" | 15.5 | 1939 | 0 | 0 | 7.30 | {} | 287 |
| Tippecanoe + | AO21 | Wilmington, California | 1-5"; 4-3" | 10.5 | 1920 | 0 | 0 | 16.8 | {} | 64 |
| Neches + | AO5 | San Francisco to Pearl Harbor | 2-5" 2-3" | 17.5 | 1918 | 0 | 0 | 22.3 | {} | 144 |
| Sunnadin | AT28 | Fleet ocean tug | 2-3".50 | 13.0 | 1919 | 0 | 0 | .79 | {} | 51 |
| Ramapo | AO12 | PH Oiler | 2-5" | 10.5 | 1919 | 0 | 0 | 16.8 | {} | 90 |
| Ontario | AT13 | Ocean tug | 2-3"/50 | 13.0 | 1912 | 0 | 0 | 1.56 | {} | 51 |
| Robin + | AM3 | 550 miles SW of Oahu | 2-3" 50 | 14.0 | 1918 | 0 | 0 | .84 | {} | 78 |
| Regulus + | AK14 | Near Midway | 2-5" | 11.5 | 1920 | 0 | 0 | 10.5 | {} | 48 |
| Argonaut + | SM1 | Near Midway: minelaying submarine | 2-6"; 4-20mm | 20.0 8.5 | 1929 | 10-21"* | 0 | 2.73 | {} | 90 |
| Wright + | AV1 | 300 miles W of Oahu | 2-5" | 15.0 | 1918 | 0 | 0 | 8.67 | {} | 288 |
| Hulbert | ADV6 | PH Seaplane tender, ex-DD | 2-3" 4-4" | 25.0 | 1920 | 0 | 0 | 1.19 | {} | 126 |
| Neosho | AO23 | PH | 1-5"; 4-3"; 8-40mm | 18.0 | 1941? | 0 | 0 | 18.25 | {} | 64 |
| Castor | AKS1 | PH | 4-5" | 15.5 | 1940 | 0 | 0 | 6.7 | {} | 315 |
| Avocet | AVP4 | PH | 1-5" 2-3" 1MG | 12.4 | 1918 | 0 | 0 | .95 | {} | 72 |
| Tangier | AV8 | PH | 2-5".38 | 17.5 | 1940 | 0 | 0 | 12.10 | {} | 1,075 |
| Utah | AG16 | PH Target ship | x | x | 1911 | x | x | | | x |
| Dobbin | AD3 | PH DD tender | 4-5"; 4-40mm | 16.0 | 1924 | 0 | 0 | 8.32 | {} | 589 |
| Solace | AH5 | PH Hospital ship | x | 18.0 | 1927 | 0 | 0 | 6.20 | {} | 568 |
| Whitney | AD4 | PH | 4-5" 4-40mm | 16.5 | 1919 | 0 | 0 | 8.32 | {} | 589 |
| Sotoyomo | YT9 | Harbor tug | 1-3; 2-40mm | 11.1 | 1919 | 0 | 0 | .26 | {} | 85 |

| Name | ID No. | Notes | Guns | Speed | Year | TT | AC | Disp | AB | Crew |
|------|--------|-------|------|-------|------|-----|-----|------|-----|------|
| **Ortolan** + | ASR5 | w/CV3 | 2-3" 50 | 14.0 | 1919 | 0 | 0 | 1.06 | {} | 79 |
| **Curtiss** | AV4 | PH | 4-5".38; 14-40mm | 19.0 | 1940 | 0 | 0 | 8.62 | {} | 1,195 |
| **Medusa** | AR1 | PH | 4-5".51; 2-3"AA | 16.0 | 1924 | 0 | 0 | 8.12 | {} | 466 |
| **Thornton** | AVD11 | PH: seaplane tender | 2-4" | 18.0 | 1919 | 0 | 0 | 1.19 | {} | {136} |
| **Pelias** | AS14 | PH: sub tender | 4-5" | 16.6 | 1941 | 0 | 0 | 7.88 | {} | 925 |
| **Sumner** | AG32 | PH: misc. auxilliary | 4-4" 1-3" | (11–15) | 1913 | 12-21" | 0 | .25 | {} | (90) |
| **Pyro** | AE1 | PH Ammunition ship | 1-5" | 17.0 | 1920 | 0 | 0 | 10.60 | {} | 289 |
| **Gillis** + | AVD12 | Yakutat Bay, Alaska | 2-4" | 25.0 | 1920 | 0 | 0 | 1.19 | {} | 120 |
| **Brazos** + | AO4 | 600 miles E of Dutch Harbor | (1-5") | 14.0 | 1919 | 0 | 0 | 14.1 | {} | (140) |
| **Richmond** + | CL9 | Off Peru | 10-6"; 8-3"; 2-3lb.; 8MG | 35.0 | 1923 | 6-21" | 2 SON1 | 7.05 | S3; UD1.5 | 458 |
| **Trenton** + | CL11 | Off Balboa | 10-6"; 8-3"; 2-3lb.; 8MGAA | 35.0 | 1920 | 6-21" | 2 SOC3 | 7.05 | S3; UD 1.5 | 458 |
| **Fulton** + | AS11 | Off Guatemala | 4-5" | 20.0 | 1938 | 0 | 0 | 9.25 | {} | (70) |
| **Gar** + | SS206 | Off Mexico | 1-4"; 2-20mm | 21.0 (8-11) | 1940 | 10-21" | 0 | 1.47 | {} | 65 |
| **Swan** | AVP7 | PH: seaplane tender | 2-3".50AA | 18.0 | 1919 | 0 | 0 | .84 | {} | 105 |
| **Vestal** | AR4 | PH: repair ship | {4-5".5 12-3"AA} | 16.0 | 1909 | 0 | 0 | 8.10 | {} | {466} |
| **Rigel** | AD13 | PH DD tender | {2-5"; 4-3"; 4-40mm} | 10.5 | 1921 | 0 | 0 | 10.0 | {} | {574} |
| **Hoga** | YT146 | PH: tug | 0 | (11.0) | 1941 | 0 | 0 | .32 | {} | (80) |
| **Cinchona** | YN7 | PH: net tender | 1-3" | 14.0 | 1941 | 0 | 0 | .70 | {} | 48 |
| **YG-17** (Garbage Scow) | YG17 | PH | 0 | | | 0 | 0 | | | |
| **YFD-2** | YFD2 | Floating dock | | | | | | | | |

# JAPANESE FLEET ORDER OF BATTLE

It is interesting to note the protocol that the Japanese Navy followed in the naming of its ships. Battleships were named after ancient provinces or mountains (4BCs). Aircraft carriers took their names from dragons or birds. Heavy cruisers were named after mountains. Light cruisers took theirs from rivers. First class destroyers were called after meteorological phenomena. Second class destroyers were named after trees, flowers, and fruits. Torpedo boats took their names from birds; and minelayers were named after islands, straits, or channels.

| Name | Transl. | Notes | Guns | Speed | Year | TT | AC | Disp | AB | Crew |
|------|---------|-------|------|-------|------|-----|-----|------|-----|------|
| **Akagi** | Red Castle | Aircraft= All, 1 red band; 1st Carrier Dlv. | 10-8" 4-4.7" 12-4.7AA | 31.5 | 1925 | 0 | (91) 27/18 Zeros 18 Vals 27 Kates | 28.1 | B T D | 2,000 |

| Name | Transl. | Notes | Guns | Speed | Year | TT | AC | Disp | AB | Crew |
|------|---------|-------|------|-------|------|-----|-----|------|-----|-------|
| **Kaga** | Increased Joy | Aircraft= AII, 2 red bands; 1st Carrier Div. | 10-8"<br>4-4.7"<br>12-4.7AA | 28.5 | 1920 | 0 | (90)<br>27/21 Zeros<br>27 Vals<br>27 Kates | 28.1 | B<br>T<br>D | 2,016 |
| **Shokaku** | IJN | Aircraft= EI, 1 white band; 3rd Carrier Div. | 12-5"AA | 34.5 | 1939 | 0 | (84)<br>15/18 Zeros<br>27 Vals<br>27 Kates | 20.0 | B<br>T<br>D | 1,660 |
| **Zuikaku** | IJN | Aircraft= EII, 2 white bands; 3rd Carrier Div. | 12-5"AA | 34.5 | 1939 | 0 | (84)<br>15/18 Zeros<br>27 Vals<br>27 Kates | 20.0 | B<br>T<br>D | 1,660 |
| **Hiryu** | Flying Dragon | Aircraft= BII, 2 blue bands; 2nd Carrier Div.; Detached to Wake | 12-5" | 34.5 | 1939 | 0 | (73)<br>24/21 Zeros<br>18/21 Vals<br>18/21 Kates | 18.8 | B<br>T<br>D | 1,100 |
| **Soryu** | Green Dragon | Aircraft= BI, 1 blue band; 2nd Carrier Div.; Detached to Wake | 12-5" | 34.5 | 1937 | 0 | (71)<br>27/18 Zeros<br>18 Vals<br>18 Kates | 18.8 | B<br>T<br>D | 1,100 |
| **Hiei** | IJN | 3rd BB Div. Aircraft: CIV | 8-14"-45<br>16-6"-50<br>8-5"AA<br>4MG | 27.5 | 1911 | 4-21" | 3<br>Daves | 29.3 | B3-10<br>D2.5-7<br>T6-9 | 1,221 |
| **Kirishima** | IJN | 3rd BB Div. Aircraft: CIII | 8-14"-45<br>16-6"-50<br>8-5"AA<br>4MG | 27.5 | 1925 | 4-21" | 3<br>Daves | 29.3 | B3-10<br>D2.5-7<br>T6-9 | 1,221 |
| **Chikuma** | IJN | Detached to Wake; Aircraft= JII | 8-8"<br>8-5"AA<br>12MG | 35.5 | 1939 | 12-21" | (5) 4<br>1 Jake<br>3 Daves | 8.5 | D2<br>S2 | 850 |
| **Tone** | IJN | Detached to Wake; Aircraft= JI | 8-8"<br>8-5"AA<br>12MG | 35.5 | 1938 | 12-21" | (5) 4<br>1 Jake<br>3 Daves | 8.5 | D2<br>S2 | 850 |
| **Abukuma** | IJN | Omori's flagship; 1st DD Sqdn Aircraft= DI | 7-5.5" | 36.0 | 1925 | 8-21" | (1)<br>2 Alfs | 5.17 | S2,T2 | 438 |
| **Katori** | IJN | Aircraft= SI | 4-5.5"<br>2-5"AA | 18.0 | 1940 | 8-21" | (1)<br>2 Alfs | 5.80 | D2 | {425} |
| **Akigumo** | Clouds | | 6-5" 4-25mm | 35.0 | 1941 | 8-24" | 0 | 2.07 | D2 | 228 |
| **Arare** | Hail | Escort to 2nd Supply Train | 6-5" 2MG | 34.0 | 1939 | 8-24" | 0 | 1.5 | {} | 200 |
| **Hamakaze** | Beach Breeze | 17th DD Sqdn | 6-5"<br>2MG | 36.0 | 1941 | 8-21" | 0 | 2.0 | {} | 240 |
| **Isokaze** | Shore Breeze | 17th DD Sqdn | 6-5" 2MG | 35.0 | 1939 | 8-24" | 0 | 2.0 | {} | 240 |
| **Kagero** | Gossamer | | 6-5" 2MG | 36.0 | 1939 | 8-24" | 0 | 2.0 | {} | 240 |
| **Kasumi** | Haze | | 6-5" 2MG | 34.0 | 1937 | 6-24" | 0 | 1.5 | {} | 190 |
| **Sazanami** | Ripples | Midway Attack Unit | 6-5" 2MG | 34.0 | 1932 | 9-24" | AC | 2.09 | {} | 197 |
| **Shiranuhi** | Phosphorescent Foam | | 6-5" 2MG | 36.0 | 1939 | 8-24" | 0 | 2.0 | {} | 240 |
| **Tanikaze** | Wind in the Valley | 17th DD Sqdn; Detached to Wake | 6-5" 2MG | 36.0 | 1941 | 8-21" | 0 | 2.0 | {} | 240 |
| **Urakazi** | Wind in the Bay | 17th DD Sqdn; Detached to Wake | 6-5" 2MG | 28.0 | 1929 | 8-21" | 0 | 2.0 | {} | (200) |
| **Ushio** | Tide | 7th DD Div. Midway Attack Unit | 6-5"<br>4MG | 38.0 | 1931 | 9-21" | 0 | (1.5) | {} | 197 |
| **I-1** | IJN | 2nd SS Sqdn; Raid and blockade Oahu | 2-5.5"<br>8.0 | 18.0<br>8.0 | 1924 | 6-21"<br>/20 | 0 | 2.13 | {} | 92 |
| **I-2** | IJN | 2nd SS Sqdn | 2-5.5"<br>8.0 | 18.0<br>8.0 | 1925 | 6-21"<br>/20 | 0 | 2.13 | {} | 92 |
| **I-3** | IJN | 2nd SS Sqdn | 2-5.5"<br>8.0 | 18.0<br>8.0 | 1925 | 6-21"<br>/20 | 0 | 2.13 | {} | 92 |
| **I-4** | IJN | 2nd SS Sqdn | 2-5.5"<br>8.0 | 18.0<br>8.0 | 1925 | 6-21"<br>/20 | 0 | 2.13 | {} | 92 |

| Name | Transl. | Notes | Guns | Speed | Year | TT | AC | Disp | AB | Crew |
|------|---------|-------|------|-------|------|-----|-----|------|-----|------|
| I-5 | IJN | 1st SS Sqdn; Raid and blockade Oahu | 2-5.5" | 18.0 8.0 | 1925 | 6-21" /20 | 0 | 2.23 | {} | 93 |
| I-6 | IJN | 2nd SS Sqdn | 1-5 1-13mm | 20.0 8.0 | 1935 | 6-21" /17 | 1 Glen | 2.24 | {} | 97 |
| I-7 | IJN | 2nd SS Sqdn | 1-5.5" 5-13mm | 23.0 8.0 | 1937 | 6-21" /20 | 1 Glen | 2.52 | {} | 100 |
| I-8 | IJN | 3rd SS Sqdn; Raid and blockade Oahu | 1-5.5" 5-13mm | 23.0 8.0 | 1938 | 6-21" /20 | 1 Glen | 2.52 | {} | 100 |
| I-9 | IJN | 1st SS Sqdn Cape Blanco to Guadelupe | 1-5.5" 4-25mm | 23.5 8.0 | 1939 | 6-21" /18 | 1 Glen | 2.43 | {} | 114 |
| I-10 | IJN | Recon and gather info: San Diego | 1-5.5" 4-25mm | 23.5 8.0 | 1939 | 6-21" /18 | 1 Glen | 2.43 | {} | 114 |
| I-15 | IJN | 1st SS Sqdn Off San Francisco | 1-5.5" 2-25mm | 23.6 8.0 | 1938 | 8-21"/17 | 1 Glen | 2.58 | {} | 101 |
| I-16 | IJN | Special Attack Unit; transport two-man subs | 1-5.5" 4-25mm | 23.6 8.0 | 1940 | 8-21"/20 | 0 | 2.55 | {} | 101 |
| I-16A | IJN | two-man sub | | 23.0 19 | 1940 | 2-18" | 0 | .46 | {} | 2 |
| I-17 | IJN | 1st SS Sqdn Cape Mendicino to San Francisco | 1-5.5" 2-25mm | 23.6 8.0 | 1939 | 6-21" /17 | 1 Glen | 2.58 | {} | 101 |
| I-18 | IJN | Special Attack Unit; transport two-man subs | 1-5.5" 4-25mm | 23.6 8.0 | 1939 | 8-21" /20 | 0 | 2.55 | {} | 101 |
| I-18A | IJN | Two-man sub | | 23.0 19 | 1939 | 2-18" | 0 | .46 | {} | 2 |
| I-19 | IJN | Recon in shipping lanes: Los Angeles to San Pedro Bay | 1-5.5" 2-25mm | 23.6 8.0 | 1939 | 6-21" /17 | 1 Glen | 2.58 | {} | 101 |
| I-20 | IJN | Special Attack Unit; transport two-man subs | 1-5.5." 2-25mm | 23.6 8.0 | 1939 | 8-21" /20 | 1 Glen | 2.55 | {} | 101 |
| I-20A | IJN | Two-man sub | | 23.0 19 | 1939 | 2-18" | 0 | .46 | {} | 2 |
| I-21 | IJN | Recon in shipping lanes Estero Point to Point Arguello | 1-5.5" 2-25mm | 23.6 8.0 | 1939 | 6-21" /17 | 1 Glen | 2.58 | {} | 101 |
| I-22 | IJN | Special Attack Unit; transport two-man subs | 1-5.5" 2-25mm | 23.6 8.0 | 1939 | 8-21" | 0/20 | 2.58 | {} | 101 |
| I-22A | IJN | Two-man sub | | 23.0 19 | 1939 | 2-18" | 0 | .46 | {} | 2 |
| I-23 | IJN | Recon in shipping lanes: off Monterey Bay | 1-5.5" 2-25mm | 23.6 8.0 | 1939 | 6-21" /42 | 1 Glen | 2.58 | {} | 101 |
| I-24 | IJN | Special Attack Unit; transport two-man subs | 1-5.5" 2-25mm | 23.6 8.0 | 1939 | 8-21" /42 | 0 | 2.58 | {} | 101 |
| I-24A | IJN | Two-man sub | | 23.0 19 | 1939 | 2-18" | 0 | .46 | {} | 2 |
| I-25 | IJN | 1st SS Sqdn Portland to Estero Bay | 1-4.7" 2-25mm | 23.6 8.0 | 1939 | 6-21" /42 | 1 Glen | 2.58 | {} | 101 |
| I-26 | IJN | Recon and gather info off Seattle | 1.5" 2-25mm | 14.5 8.0 | 1939 | 6-21" /42 | 1 Glen | 2.19 | {} | 94 |
| I-68 | IJN | 3rd SS Sqdn | 1-3.9" 1-13mm | 23.0 8.0 | 1933 | 6-21" /14 | 0 | 1.4 | {} | 79 |
| I-69 | IJN | 3rd SS Sqdn | 1-3.9" 1-13mm | 23.0 8.2 | 1934 | 6-21" /14 | 0 | 1.4 | {} | 60–84 |
| I-70 | IJN | 3rd SS Sqdn | 1-3.9" 1-13mm | 23.0 8.2 | 1934 | 6-21" /14 | 0 | 1.4 | {} | 82–84 |
| I-71 | IJN | 3rd SS Sqdn | 1-4.7" 1-13mm | 23.0 8.2 | 1934 | 6-21" /14 | 0 | 1.4 | {} | 82–84 |
| I-72 | IJN | 3rd SS Sqdn | 1-4.7" 1-13mm | 23.0 8.2 | 1935 | 6-21" /14 | 0 | 1.4 | {} | 82–84 |

# Japanese fleet order of battle continued

| Name | Transl. | Notes | Guns | Speed | Year | TT | AC | Disp | AB | Crew |
|------|---------|-------|------|-------|------|-----|-----|------|-----|------|
| I-73 | IJN | 3rd SS Sqdn | 1-4.7"<br>1-13mm | 23.0<br>8.2 | 1935 | 6-21"<br>/14 | 0 | 1.4 | {} | 82–84 |
| I-74 | IJN | 3rd SS Sqdn | 1-4.7"<br>1-13mm | 23.0<br>8.2 | 1937 | 6-21"<br>/14 | 0 | 1.4 | {} | 82–84 |
| I-75 | IJN | 3rd SS Sqdn | 1-4.7"<br>1-13mm | 23.0<br>8.2 | 1936 | 6-21"<br>/14 | 0 | 1.4 | {} | 82–84 |
| Kenyo Maru | Oiler | 1st Supply Train | 2-5.5" | 19.0 | 1939 | 0 | 0 | (9.0) | {} | {160} |
| Kokuyo Maru | Oiler | 1st Supply Train | 2-5.5" | 19.0 | 1939 | 0 | 0 | 10.05 | {} | {160} |
| Kyokuto Maru | Oiler | Flagship; 1st Supply Train | 2-5.5" | 19.0 | 1934 | 0 | 0 | 10.0 | {} | {160} |
| Nihon (Nippon) Maru | Oiler | 2nd Supply Train | 2-5.5" | 19.0 | 1936 | 0 | 0 | 9.97 | {} | {160} |
| Shinkoku Maru | Oiler | 1st Supply Train | 2-5.5" | 18.5 | 1940 | 0 | 0 | (9.0) | {} | {160} |
| Toei Maru | Oiler | 2nd Supply Train | 2-5.5" | 16.0 | 1938 | 0 | 0 | 10.02 | {} | {160} |
| Toho Maru | Oiler | Flagship; 2nd Supply Train | 2-5.5" | 19.0 | 1936 | 0 | 0 | 9.98 | {} | {160} |
| Shiriya | Oiler | 2nd Supply Train | 2-5.5" | 16.0 | 1920 | 0 | 0 | 14.05 | {} | 157 |

**CHART KEY**

**Name** = Name of vessel
**Transl.** = Name translation, or ship type
**Notes** = Class of vessel, plus location
**Guns** = Size and caliber of main armament
**Speed** = Surface speed in knots of vessel
**Year** = Year completed or commissioned
**TT** = Torpedo tubes and size of torpedo; reloads follows slash
**AC** = Aircraft carried

**( )** = AC assigned, followed by those present and a '/' separates those present and possibly on CAP from those listed second which participated in attack
**Disp** = Displacement in tons
**AB** = Armor (B:belt, S:side, T:turrets and gun positions, UD:upper deck, MD = main deck)
**Crew** = Assigned crew members
  **{ }** = Estimated, based on available records
*Aircraft in notes* = ID No. of aircraft and markings

RIGHT **In pre-war Hawaii soldiers led a routine life. Many on guard duty walked their tour in Class As with highly polished brass, white gloves, and chin straps instead of fatigues. On 7 December 1941 this changed.**

# JAPANESE AIRCRAFT AT PEARL HARBOR

| Aircraft name and designation | SVC | Armament | Bomb or torpedo payload | Crew | Speed and range | Description |
|-------------------------------|-----|----------|-------------------------|------|-----------------|-------------|
| Aichi 3A2 Val Type 99, Model 22 | Navy | 1-2 x 7.7mm sync MG over engine and 1 x 7.7mm MG in rear cockpit | 1 x 250kg bomb pivots under fusilage and 1 x 60kg bomb under each wing | 2 back to back | 281 mph 874 miles | Carrier borne, single-engine dive-bomber Fixed landing gear |
| Mitsubishi A6M5 Zeke or Zero Model 11 | Navy | 2 x 7.7mm sync MG in cowling and 2 x 20mm cannons in wings | 1 x 60kg under each wing | 1 | 340 mph 1,160 miles | Fighter, retractable landing gear, carrier borne |
| Aichi E13A1/a/b Jake | Navy | 1 x forward firing 7.7mm MG & 1 x 20mm cannon | 1 x 250kg or 4 x 60kg bombs | 3 | 203 knots 1,200 miles | 3-man, low-wing monoplane, floatplane |
| Nakajima E8N1/2 Dave | Navy | 1 x forward firing 7.7mm MG, 1 x flexible 7.7mm MG | 2 x 66lb or 1 x 132lb bombs | 2 | 184 mph 750–900 miles | 2-man biplane, floatplane |
| Hikoki E7K2 Alf | Navy | 1 x forward firing 7.7mm MG; 2 x flexible 7.7mm MG | 4 x 132lb bombs | 3 | 171 mph 1,147 miles | 3-man biplane, twin-float plane |
| Yokosuka E14Y1 Glen | Navy | 1 x 7.7mm MG | 2 x 110lb bombs | 2 | 153 mph 548 miles | 2-man submarine borne floatplane monoplane |
| Nakajima B5N2 Kate Type 97, Model 12 | Navy | 2 x 7.7mm MG in cowling; 1-2 x 7.7mm MG x 1 in rear cockpit | 1 x 18in. torpedo or 1 x 500kg bomb | 2–3 | 225 mph 683 miles | Single-engine torpedo bomber, retractable landing gear |

# US AIRCRAFT AT PEARL HARBOR

| Aircraft name and designation | SVC | Armament | Bomb or torpedo payload | Crew | Speed and range | Description |
|---|---|---|---|---|---|---|
| Vought Sikorsky SB2U Vindicator | Navy | 4 x .30-cal. MG; 1 x .30-cal. MG rear cockpit | 1 x 1,000lb bomb | 2 | 257 mph 700 miles | Single-engine, two-seat scout and dive-bomber |
| Douglas RD-4 Dolphin OA-3/4 | Army | | | 2–3 | 140 mph 660 miles | Twin engine observation amphibian |
| Grumman J4F-1 Widgeon | Navy | 1 x depth charge (stbd) | | 3 | 150 mph 780 miles | Twin engine amphibian |
| Grumman J2F Duck | Navy | 1 x .30-cal. flexible MG in rear cockpit | 2 x 100lb bombs or 2 x 325lb depth charges | 2 | 155 mph 675 miles | Two-seat biplane single-float amphibian |
| North American 0-47 | Army | 1 x .30-cal. MG in wing; 1 x flexible .30-cal. MG | N/A | 3 | 221 mph 700 miles | Observation plane |
| Martin B-12A | Army | 3 x .30-cal. MG | 2,260lb bomb load | 4–5 | 213 mph 700 miles | Twin-engine medium land-based bomber |
| B-17B and B17D Flying Fortress | Army | 13 x .50-cal. MG | 6,000lb bomb bay capacity | 6–10 | 295 mph 1,100 miles | Four-engine bomber |
| P-40 Warhawk (aka Tomahawk etc.) | Army | 3 x .50-cal. MG on each wing | 1 x 100lb or 600lb bomb under fusilage and wing racks to carry 2 x 100–500lb bombs | 1 | 364 mph 610 or 1,200 miles with belly tank | Fighter |
| Consolidated PBY5 Catalina flying boat | Navy | Browning MG in blister on each side | Bombs or depth charges under wings | 10 | 194 mph 2,520 miles | Bomber, ASW, rescue, two-engine floatplane or land aircraft |
| P-36A Curtiss Hawk | Army | 1 x .50-cal. and 3 x .30-cal. MG | N/A | 1 | 323 mph 625 miles | Fighter |
| Chance Voight OS2U Kingfisher | Navy | 1 x .30-cal. sync MG in cowling; 1 x .30-cal. MG for rear observer | Wing carried 2 x 100lb or 8 x 30lb bombs | 2 | 171 mph 908 miles | Observation seaplane |
| P-26 Peashooter | Army | 1 x .30-cal. MG; 1 x .50-cal. MG | 2 x 100kg bombs | 1 | 234 mph 570 miles | Pursuit plane, fixed landing gear, single seat monoplane |
| Douglas TBD-1 Devastator | Navy | 1 x .30-cal. MG; 1 x .50-cal. MG | 1 x 21in. torpedo; 1 x 1,000lb bomb | 3 | 206 mph 716 miles | Monoplane torpedo dive-bomber |
| Douglas SBD2 Dauntless | Navy | 1 x .50-cal. MG in fusilage; 1 x .30-cal. MG in rear position | 1 x 1,000lb bomb pivot cradle; 2 x 100lb bombs beneath wings | 2 | 255 mph 1,345 miles | Scout monoplane dive-bomber |
| A-20 Douglas Havoc | Army | 2 x .50-cal. MG turret; 1 x .50-cal. flexible 1 x .30-cal. flexible MG MG upper;  lower (2 x .30-cal. rear-firing MG in nacelle) | 1 x 2,000lb naval torpedo or bombs | 3–4 | 325 mph c.1,500 miles | Bomber |
| Douglas B-18 Bolo | Army | 3 x .30-cal. MG | 4,000lb bomb load | 6 | 217 mph 1,082 miles | Twin engine heavy bomber |
| F4F-3 Wildcat | Marines and Navy | 4 x .50-cal. MG | 2 x 100lb bombs | 1 | 318mph 1,150 miles | Only carrier borne Navy monoplane fighter at start of WWII |
| Curtis SOC-1, 2, 3 and 4 Seagull | Navy | 2 x .30-cal. MG | 2 x 100lb bombs | 2 | 165 mph 625 miles | Folding wing biplane scout |

# JAPANESE FIRST WAVE ATTACK FORMATION

| Group, carrier of origin, and unit | Aircraft types | Armament | Mission | Division commander | Overall commander |
|---|---|---|---|---|---|
| **FIRST GROUP** | | | | | |
| **1st Attack Unit** *Akagi* (Aircraft tail ID: AI-) | 5 Kates 5 Kates 5 Kates | 800kg AP bomb | *Maryland* *Tennessee* or *West Virgina* *Tennessee* or *West Virgina* | **1st** Lt.Cmdr Mitsuo Fuchida **2nd** Lt. Goro Iwasaki **3rd** Lt. Izumi Furukawa | Lt.Cmdr Mitsuo Fuchida (AI-301) |
| **2nd Attack Unit** *Kaga* (Aircraft tail ID: AII-) | 5 Kates 5 Kates 4 Kates | 800kg AP bomb | *Tennessee* or *West Virgina* *Arizona/Vestal* *Tennessee* or *West Virgina* | **1st** Lt.Cmdr Takahashi Hashiguchi **2nd** Lt. Hideo Maki **3rd** Lt. Yoshitaka Mikami | Lt.Cmdr. Takahashi Hashiguchi (AII-201) |
| **3rd Attack Unit** *Soryu* (Aircraft tail ID: BI-) | 5 Kates 5 Kates | 800kg AP bomb | *Tennessee* or *West Virgina* *Nevada* | **1st** Lt. Heijiro Abe **2nd** Lt. Sadao Yamamoto | Lt. Heijiro Abe |
| **4th Attack Unit** *Hiryu* (Aircraft tail ID: BII-) | 5 Kates 5 Kates | 800kg AP bomb | *Arizona* *California* | **1st** Lt.Cmdr Tadashi Kusumi **2nd.** Lt. Toshio Hashimoto | Lt.Cmdr Tadashi Kusumi |
| **1st Torpedo Attack Unit** *Akagi* | 6 Kates 6 Kates | Mk 91 aerial torpedo | *West Virginia* or *Oklahoma* *California*, *West Virginia* or *Oklahoma* | **4th** Lt.Cmdr Shigeharu Murata **5th** Lt. Asao Negishi | Lt.Cmdr Shigeharu Murata (AI-311) |
| **2nd Torpedo Attack Unit** *Kaga* | 6 Kates 6 Kates | Mk 91 aerial torpedo | *West Virginia* or *Oklahoma* *West Virginia*, *Nevada,* or *Oklahoma* | **1st** Lt. Kazuyoshi Kitajima **2nd** Lt. Mimori Suzuki | Lt. Kazuyoshi Kitajima (AII-311) |
| **3rd Torpedo Attack Unit** *Soryu* | 4 Kates 4 Kates | Mk 91 aerial torpedo | *California*, *Utah* or *Helena* *Raleigh*, *Utah* | **1st** Lt. Tsuyoshi Nagai **2nd** Lt. Tatsumi Nakajima | Lt. Tsuyoshi Nagai (BI-311) |
| **4rd Torpedo Attack Unit** *Hiryu* | 4 Kates 4 Kates | Mk 91 aerial torpedo | *West Virginia* or *Oklahoma* *Helena* | **1st** Lt. Heita Matsumura **2nd** Lt. Hiruharo Sumino | Lt. Heita Matsumura (BII-320) |
| **SECOND GROUP** | | | | | |
| **15th Attack Unit** *Shokaku* (Aircraft tail ID: EI-) | 9 Vals 8 Vals 9 Vals | 250kg general purpose dive-bomb | NAS Pearl Harbor Hickam Field Hickam Field | **1st** Lt. Masao Yamaguchi **2nd** Lt. Hisayoshi Fujita **3rd** Lt.Cmdr Kakuichi Takahashi | Lt. Cmdr Kakuichi Takahashi (EI-238) |
| **16th Attack Unit** *Zuikaku* (Aircraft tail ID: EII-) | 9 Vals 6 Vals (est.) 10 Vals (est.) | 250kg general purpose dive-bomb | Wheeler Field Wheeler Field Wheeler Field | **1st** Lt. Akira Sakamoto **2nd** Lt. Tomatsu Ema **3rd** Lt. Hayashi | Lt. Akira Sakamoto (EII-201) |
| **THIRD GROUP** | | | | | |
| **1st Fighter Combat Unit** *Akagi* | 9 Zeros | 20mm cannon and 7.7mm MG | Hickam Field and Ewa MACS Air control and strafing grounded aircraft at Ford Island and Hickam Field | **2nd** Lt. Cmdr Shigeru Itaya | Lt.Cmdr Shigeru Itaya (AI-155) |
| **2nd Fighter Combat Unit** *Kaga* | 9 Zeros | 20mm cannon and 7.7mm MG | Hickam Field and Ford Island Air control and strafing grounded aircraft at Ford Island and Hickam Field | **1st** Lt. Yoshio Shiga | Lt. Yoshio Shiga (AII-105) |
| **3rd Fighter Combat Unit** *Soryu* | 8 Zeros | 20mm cannon and 7.7mm MG | Wheeler Field and Ewa MACS Air control and strafing grounded aircraft at Wheeler Field and Barbers Point | **3rd** Lt. Masaji Suganami | Lt. Masaji Suganami |
| **4th Fighter Combat Unit** *Hiryu* | 6 Zeros | 20mm cannon and 7.7mm MG | Wheeler Field and Ewa MACS Air Control and strafing grounded aircraft at Wheeler Field and Barber's Point | **4th** Lt. Kiyokima Okajima | Lt. Kiyokima Okajima (BII-110) |
| **5th Fighter Combat Unit** *Shokaku* | 6 Zeros | 20mm cannon | NAS Kaneohe and Bellows Field. Air control and strafing grounded aircraft at Kaneohe | **5th** Lt. Tadashi Kaneko | Lt. Tadashi Kaneko (EI-101) |
| **6th Fighter Combat Unit** *Zuikaku* | 5 Zeros | 20mm cannon and 7.7mm MG | NAS Kaneohe Air control and strafing grounded aircraft at Kaneohe | **6th** Lt. Masao Sato | Lt. Masao Sato (EII-137) |

# JAPANESE SECOND WAVE ATTACK FORMATION

| Group, carrier of origin, and unit | Aircraft types | Armament | Mission | Division commander | Overall commander |
|---|---|---|---|---|---|
| **FIRST GROUP** | | | | | Lt.Cmdr Shigekazu Shimazaki |
| **5th Attack Unit** *Shokaku* Aircraft tail ID EI- | 9 Kates 9 Kates 9 Kates | 1 x 250kg general purpose bomb and 6 x 60kg regular bombs, or 2 x 250kg bombs for high altitude bombing | Kaneohe NAS Kaneohe NAS NAS Pearl Harbor | **1st** Lt. Tatsuo Ichihara **2nd** Lt. Tsutomu Hagiwara **3rd** Lt. Yoshiaki Ikuin | Lt. Tatsuo Ichihara |
| **6th Attack Unit** *Zuikaku* Aircraft tail ID EII- | 9 Kates 9 Kates 9 Kates | 1 x 250kg general purpose bomb and 6 x 60kg regular bombs, or 2 x 250kg bombs for high altitude bombing | Hickam Field Hickam Field Hickam Field | **1st** Lt.Cmdr Shigekazu Shimazaki **2nd** Lt. Takemi Iwami **3rd** Lt. Yoshiaki Subota | Lt.Cmdr Shigekazu Shimazaki |
| **SECOND GROUP** | | | | | Lt.Cmdr Takashige Egusa |
| **13th Attack Unit** *Akagi* Aircraft tail ID AI- | 9 Vals 9 Vals | 250kg general purpose dive-bomb | Ford Island NW, *Neosho*, *Shaw* Ford Island NW, *Nevada* | **1st** Lt. Takehiko Chihaya **2nd** Lt. Zenji Abe | Lt.Takehiko Chihaya |
| **14th Attack Unit** *Hiryu* Aircraft tail ID BII- | 8 Vals 9 Vals | 250kg general purpose dive-bomb | Navy Yard, *California* and *Maryland* *West Virginia* | **1st** Lt. Michio Kobayashi **2nd** Lt. Shun Nakagawa | Lt. Michio Kobayashi (unable to fly due to engine trouble) |
| **11th Attack Unit** *Soryu* Aircraft tail ID BI- | 9 Vals 8 Vals | 250kg general purpose dive-bomb | Navy Yard, *California* Navy Yard, *California*, *Raleigh* | **1st** Lt.Cmdr Takashige Egusa **2nd** Lt. Masatake Ikeda | Lt.Cmdr Takashige Egusa (BI-231) |
| **12th Attack Unit** *Kaga* Aircraft tail ID AII- | 8 Vals 9 Vals 9 Vals | 250kg general purpose dive-bomb | *Nevada* *Maryland*, *West Virginia*, *Nevada* *Nevada* | **1st** Lt. Saburo Makino **2nd** Lt. Shoichi Ogawa **3rd** Lt. Shoichi Ibuki | Lt. Saburo Makino (AII-240) |
| **THIRD GROUP** | | | | | Lt. Saburo Shindo |
| **1st Fighter Combat Unit** *Akagi* Aircraft tail ID AI- | 9 Zeros | 20mm cannon and 7.7mm MG | Hickam Field | **1st** Lt. Saburo Shindo | Lt. Saburo Shindo (AI-201) |
| **2nd Fighter Combat Unit** *Kaga* Aircraft tail ID AII- | 9 Zeros | 20mm cannon and 7.7mm MG | Pearl Harbor | **2nd** Lt. Yasushi Nikaido | Lt. Yasushi Nikaido (AII-121) |
| **3rd Fighter Combat Unit** *Soryu* Aircraft tail ID BI- | 9 Zeros | 20mm cannon and 7.7mm MG | NAS Kaneohe | **3rd** Lt. Fusata Iida | Lt. Fusata Iida (BI-151) |
| **4th Fighter Combat Unit** *Hiryu* Aircraft tail ID BII- | 9 Zeros | 20mm cannon and 7.7mm MG | NAS Kaneohe and Bellows Field | **4th** Lt. Sumio Nono | Lt. Sumio Nono |

**Schofield Barracks stood three stories tall and was among the prime army targets singled out by the Japanese. Surrounded by parade grounds, Schofield was easy for attackers to target.**

# JAPANESE ORGANIZATION

| Prime Minister |
|---|
| Gen. Hideki Tojo |

| Japanese Combined Fleet Commander-in-Chief |
|---|
| Adm. Isoroku Yamamoto |

| 1st Air Fleet C-in-C / Commander Hawaii Operation |
|---|
| V.Adm. Chuichi Nagumo |

| 1st Carrier Div. | 2nd Carrier Div. | 3rd Carrier Div. |
|---|---|---|
| *Akagi , Kaga* | *Soryu, Hiryu* | *Shokaku, Zuikaku* |

| 1st Destroyer Sqdn Commander: R.Adm. Sentaro Omori | 3rd Battleship Div. Commander: V.Adm. Gunichi Mikawa | 2nd Submarine Div.Commander: Cpt. Kijiro Imaizumi | 7th Destroyer Div. Commander: Cpt. Kaname Ohishi |
|---|---|---|---|
| **1st Destroyer Sqdn** *Abukuma* 17th Destroyer Sqdn *Tanikaze, Urakaze, Isokaze, Hamakaze* | **3rd BB Div.** *Hiei, Kirishima* | **2nd Sub. Div.** *I-19, I-21, I-23* | **7th Destroyer Div.** *Akebono, Ushio* |

| 1st Supply Train |
|---|
| Cpt. Masanao Oto |
| *Kyokuto Maru, Kenyo Maru, Kokuyo Maru, Shinkoku Maru* |

| 2nd Supply Train |
|---|
| Cpt. Kazutaka |
| *Niimi Toei Maru, Toho Maru, Nihon Maru, Shiriya* |

Units working in conjunction with Hawaii Operation

| Sixth Submarine Fleet |
|---|
| V.Adm. Mitsumi Shimizu (*Katori,* flagship of 6th SS fleet) |

| 1st Squadron R.Adm. | 2nd Squadron | 3rd Squadron |
|---|---|---|
| Tsutomu Sato *I-9, I-15, I-17, I-25* Mission: raid and blockade Oahu | R.Adm. Shigeaki Yazazaki *I-1, I-2, I-3, I-4, I-5, I-6, I-7* Mission: raid and blockade Oahu | R.Adm. Shigeoshi Miwa *I-8, I-68, I-69, I-70, I-71, I-72, I-73, I-74, I-75* Mission: raid and blockade Oahu |

| Special Attack Unit | Recon |
|---|---|
| Cpt. Hanku Sasaki *I-16, I-18, I-20, I-22, I-24* Special Attack Unit submarines all carried midget 2-man submarines | Cmdr Yasuchika Kashihara *I-10, I-26* Mission: intelligence gathering and recon |

# US ORGANIZATION
7 December 1941

| War Department |
|---|
| Secretary of War: Henry L. Stimson |

| Chief of Staff |
|---|
| Gen. Geo. C. Marshall |

| DCS / General Admin. and Ground Forces Maj.Gen. W. Bryden | DCS / Army Forces and Supply Maj.Gen. R.C. Moore | DCS / Air Maj.Gen. H.H. Arnold |
|---|---|---|

| G-1 Personnel | G-2 Intelligence Brig.Gen. Sherman Miles | G-3 Operations and Training | G-4 Supply Adjutant | The Judge Advocate General |
|---|---|---|---|---|
| | Counter Intelligence Lt.Col. J. T. Bissell | War Plans Division Brig.Gen. L.T. Gerow | Chief Signal Officer Maj.Gen. D. Olmstead | |
| | Intelligence Col. H.A. Kroner | | Operations Col. O.K. Sadtler | |
| | Far Eastern Section Col. R.S. Bratton | | Traffic and Signal Center Col. E.T. French | |
| | Japan Lt.Col. C.C. Dusenbury, 2nd-Lt. J.B. Schinde | | Signal Intelligence Service Col. R.W. Minckler | |
| | | | Principal Cryptanalyst W.F. Friedman | |

## Navy Department

| Secretary of the Navy |
|---|
| Frank Knox |

| Chief of Naval Operations |
|---|
| Adm. H.R. Stark |

| CinCPAC |
|---|
| Adm. H. Kimmel |

| Commandant 14th Naval District |
|---|
| Commander Hawaiian Naval Coastal Frontier Pearl Harbor Navy Yard R.Adm. R.C. Bloch (Commander Task Force Four) |

| Chief of Staff |
|---|
| Cpt. J.B. Earle |

| Intelligence Officer | Communications Security-Intelligence |
|---|---|
| Cpt. I.H. Mayfield | Cmdr J.J. Rochefort |

| Commander Naval Base Defense Air Force Commander Task Force Nine Commander Hawaiian Patrol Wing and Patrol Wing Two |
|---|
| R.Adm. P.N.L. Bellinger |

LEFT **After Pearl Harbor the Japanese reconstructed the harbor and Battleship Row to how it was just prior to the attack – for use in a motion picture. Captured after the war, R.Adm. Shafroth gave Adm. Nimitz this photo.**

## Hawaiian Army Command

| Commanding officer |
|---|
| Lt.Gen. Walter C. Short |

| Chief of Staff |
|---|
| Col. W.C. Phillips |

| G-1 Personnel | G-2 Intelligence | G-3 Operations and Training | G-4 Supply |
|---|---|---|---|
| Lt.Col. R.C. Throckmorton | Lt.Col. K.J. Fiedler | Lt.Col. W.E. Donegan | Col. M.W. Marston |

| Adjutant General | 24th Inf. Division |
|---|---|
| Col. R.H. Dunlop | Brig.Gen. D.S. Wilson |

| 25th Inf. Division |
|---|
| Maj.Gen. Maxwell Murray |

| Signal Corps | |
|---|---|
| Lt.Col. C.A. Powell | |

| Coast Artillery Command |
|---|
| Maj.Gen. H.T. Burgen |

## Hawaiian Army Air Force

| Hawaiian Department |
|---|
| Lt. Gen. Walter C. Short |

| Commanding officer |
|---|
| Maj.Gen. Frederick L. Martin |

| Chief of Staff |
|---|
| Col. J.A. Mollison |

| Intelligence | 18th Bombardment Wing |
|---|---|
| Col. E.W. Bailey | Brig.Gen. J.H. Rudolph |

| 14th Pursuit Wing |
|---|
| Brig.Gen. H.C. Davidson |

| Signal Officer | Hickam Field |
|---|---|
| Lt.Col. C.I. Hoppaugh | Col. W.E. Farthing |

| Wheeler Field |
|---|
| Col. W.J. Flood |

| Bellows Field |
|---|
| Lt.Col. L.D. Weddington |

## US Pacific Fleet

| Commander in Chief Pacific Fleet (CinCPAC) |
|---|
| Adm. H.E. Kimmel |

| Chief of Staff |
|---|
| Cpt. W.E. Smith |

| Operations Officer | War Plans Officer | Gunnery Officer | Communications Officer | Aviation Officer | Intelligence Officer |
|---|---|---|---|---|---|
| Cpt. W.S. Delany | Cpt. C.E. McMorris | Cmdr W.A. Kitts | Cmdr M.E. Curts | Cmdr A. Davis | Lt.Cmdr E.T. Layton |

| 1st Asst. Ops Officer | | | | | Task Force 1 |
|---|---|---|---|---|---|
| Cmdr R.F. Good | | | | | V.Adm. W.S. Pye |

| Task Force 2 |
|---|
| V.Adm. W.F. Halsey |

| Task Force 3 |
|---|
| V.Adm. W. Brown |

| Task Force 4 |
|---|
| R.Adm. C.C. Bloch |

| Task Force 7 |
|---|
| R.Adm. T. Withers |

| Task Force 9 |
|---|
| R.Adm. P.N.L. Bellinger |

| Task Force 15 |
|---|
| R.Adm. W.L. Calhoun |

---

# COMPANION SERIES FROM OSPREY

## MEN-AT-ARMS

An unrivalled source of information on the organization, uniforms and equipment of the world's fighting men, past and present. The series covers hundreds of subjects spanning 5,000 years of history. Each 48-page book includes concise texts packed with specific information, some 40 photos, maps and diagrams, and eight color plates of uniformed figures.

## ELITE

Detailed information on the uniforms and insignia of the world's most famous military forces. Each 64-page book contains some 50 photographs and diagrams, and 12 pages of full-color artwork.

## NEW VANGUARD

Comprehensive histories of the design, development and operational use of the world's armored vehicles and artillery. Each 48-page book contains eight pages of full-color artwork including a detailed cutaway.

## WARRIOR

Definitive analysis of the armor, weapons, tactics and motivation of the fighting men of history. Each 64-page book contains cutaways and exploded artwork of the warrior's weapons and armor.

## ORDER OF BATTLE

The most detailed information ever published on the units which fought history's great battles. Each 96-page book contains comprehensive organization diagrams supported by ultra-detailed color maps. Each title also includes a large fold-out base map.

## AIRCRAFT OF THE ACES

Focuses exclusively on the elite pilots of major air campaigns, and includes unique interviews with surviving aces sourced specifically for each volume. Each 96-page volume contains up to 40 specially commissioned artworks, unit listings, new scale plans and the best archival photography available.

## COMBAT AIRCRAFT

Technical information from the world's leading aviation writers on the aircraft types flown. Each 96-page volume contains up to 40 specially commissioned artworks, unit listings, new scale plans and the best archival photography available.